DEADLY DALLAS

DEADLY DALLAS

——— *A History of* ———

UNFORTUNATE INCIDENTS
& GRISLY FATALITIES

RUSTY WILLIAMS

THE
History
PRESS

Published by The History Press
Charleston, SC
www.historypress.com

Front cover, upper left: DeGolyer Library, Southern Methodist University; upper right: the University of Texas at Dallas; lower left: Hardin-Simmons University Library; lower right: Fire Museum of Texas.
Back cover, top of page: the University of Texas at Dallas.

First published 2021

Manufactured in the United States

ISBN 9781467148498

Library of Congress Control Number: 2021934582

CONTENTS

A PICTURE-BOOK PAST

O pen one of those big coffee-table books full of black-and-white photographs of Dallas history and turn to the pages showing the city at the beginning of the twentieth century. You might see impossibly ornate stone office buildings or proud mercantile owners posing in front of wooden retail establishments. Barrel-chested workmen stand atop wagons stacked with tools and materials. Men in straw boaters and women under white parasols stroll broad sidewalks, horses draw high-wheeled carriages and stolid mules pull streetcars. There may be photographs that were taken from atop the new, five-story red courthouse, showing a bustling commercial district and, near the horizon, a few miles away, quaint white farmhouses and assorted outbuildings. From that higher angle, you can see the Trinity River emerge from farmland and forest to the north, its braids winding off to the south and east.

These are glimpses of a city that, even then, was proud, confident, cosmopolitan and dynamic.

You might, from time to time, imagine stepping into those photographs. You might daydream of a life in that long-ago city that was slower, safer, less stressful. Your world would move at a horse-drawn pace, and with no electronic distractions, your social and cultural life would be richer and more satisfying.

Enjoy those daydreams, but don't believe them.

Dallas, in the years before and after the turn of the twentieth century, was a deathtrap. Just outside the frame of every one of those old photographs, sudden death lurked. Disaster, unexpected mayhem and the Grim Reaper waited around every turn. Those massive stone buildings? There were no fire escapes or fire department ladders tall enough to reach above the third floor. Most of those mercantile stores were long, narrow and dark, lamp soot and grit collected among the merchandise. Poor refrigeration at the butcher shop would have required you to trim away the rotted edges from the meat you bought there. Tradesmen—painters, plumbers, shoemakers, cleaners, furniture makers and haberdashers—used materials permeated with lead, deadly chemicals, flammable compounds or all three. At construction sites, crews fired up huge locomotive-sized steam boilers, explosive boilers that could level a city block if not adjusted continuously.

You had to take care when stepping out into the street. The beautiful carriage horses and sturdy dray animals—not to mention pigs and goats on their way to market—left the road surface a soupy mixture of urine, feces and other pestiferous liquids. But you couldn't stare too long at your high-button shoes; you risked being run over by carriages, wagons, horses, trolley cars, early automobiles and even locomotives that were competing for space on roads that, as of yet, had no traffic laws.

You weren't safe in your house, either. They were built of wood, ready to be squashed flat by a cyclone that no one could yet forecast or go up in flames if lit by an errant cinder from your neighbor's trash fire. Fire danger lurked inside homes, too. Woodstoves, gas lamps and kerosene lanterns ensured there were open flames throughout these houses. Touched by a spark, your frilly cotton clothing would burn like a straw scarecrow before you could call for help. In the shed, you'd probably store powdered rat poison, deadly to curious children. There's dynamite there, too—available from any hardware store—that you'd use to remove stumps or dig wells. For recreation, you could boat at your own risk on the Trinity River—much of the city's sewerage was dumped there.

———•———

IT'S EASY TO THINK of turn-of-the-century Dallas as a quaint and peaceable place—open carriages taking dressed-up families to park outings, the *ding-ding-ding* of hustling trollies, well-stocked retail emporiums, stolid bankers and the soft, flickering glow of gaslit streets. After all, Dallas was on the cusp of becoming a great city, an international city, the hub of a great conurbation by the end of the century. Dallas was a city beginning the process of transforming its skyline, roads, civic institutions, public behavior and sense of self and worth. In 1900, however, with a population of just forty-three thousand—more rural than urban—Dallas was still a gangly adolescent, always outgrowing its shoes and heedless of the dangers around it.

Deadly Dallas: A History of Unfortunate Incidents and Grisly Fatalities casts new light on the history of the city from the 1880s through the 1920s. It was a city more lethal than the old black-and-white photographs might suggest.

At the turn of the century, Dallas was changing from a prairie town into the metropolis it would become. The city's population and commercial growth, at times, outpaced the supply of clean drinking water or the availability of sufficient water to fight fires. Horse-drawn and motorized traffic often crowded Dallas streets and taxed the city's ability to maintain and improve them. The burgeoning population needed housing, which, at times, resulted in homes and boardinghouses that were shabbily built or dangerously overcrowded.

Even as Dallas entered the new century, it brought remnants of the old one with it: diseases for which there were no cures, the everyday use of kerosene lanterns and indoor wood-burning stoves and a river that overflowed its banks and flooded the city's lowlands. Civic water wells were equipped with dippers that could be used by any thirsty passersby, a sure way to spread deadly diseases.

The twentieth century brought new technologies (which brought problems of their own). Gas lighting was an improvement over oil lamps, but the installation of gas lines by unlicensed handymen and the lack of city inspection could result in explosive tragedies for businesses and homes. Plodding mule cars were replaced by faster and heavier electric trolleys, which were quieter and harder to stop.

Area newspapers reported in graphic language the results of the city's changes: stories of unfortunate incidents, deplorable mayhem and grisly fatalities. Describing a man maimed in a trolley collision, a newspaper told readers he "was sliced into two parts across the middle, as if by a sharp knife." Another newspaper reported that a woman trapped in a burning building was "roasted to death as she cried piteously for release from the fiery wreckage." Not exactly what you'd want to read today while sipping your morning coffee. However, such stories shed light on problems brought about by growth, urbanization and new technologies in Dallas at the turn of the century. Reports of fires, explosions, collisions, drownings, cyclones and other tragic occurrences—including some murders, suicides and dangerous public entertainments—illustrate the nature and character of city life during that transitional time.

Twenty-first-century Dallas has experienced many of the same calamities: gas explosions, fires, tornados, floods and contagion. The unfortunate incidents, deplorable mayhem and grisly fatalities of *Deadly Dallas* may, at times, read less like history and more like current events.

Step back to a time when death—sudden and unexpected or slow and excruciating—could come in ways your twenty-first-century self would never expect. A pale horse galloped the streets and alleys of turn-of-the-century Dallas, and the true stories you're about to read prove it.

DEADLY DALLAS TRAFFIC

Maybe you've imagined clip-clopping alongside tree-shaded Turtle Creek in a decorated carriage drawn by matched high-stepping strutters. Perhaps an elegant hansom cab is more your style. Or a two-wheeled "sweetheart cart." For something more modern, try looking into shop windows on a leisurely drive down Main Street in your 1912 Buick 35 with leather upholstery.

Sound comfortable, relaxing and safe? You'd be dead wrong.

Traveling the streets of turn-of-the-century Dallas could be as harrowing as a blindfolded rush hour trip up the length of Dallas North Tollway today—or worse.

From the 1880s through much of the 1920s, all manner of vehicles shared the streets of Dallas: horse-drawn and mule-drawn, two-wheel gigs and four-wheel carriages, streetcars, delivery wagons, bicycles, locomotives and (later) jitneys, automobiles, autotrucks and motorcycles. At the time, there were few enforceable rules of the road.

A dynamic city requires food and clothing, with bulk deliveries of merchandise, and that people—mounted and dismounted—have access to the city center in order to buy those goods or partake of its services. But Dallas's dynamism often outstripped its ability to move people and goods into and out of the city center. The result could be injury, dismemberment or death.

As you look at those early photographs of downtown Dallas streets, notice that they were not paved—they were packed dirt, slotted by the iron wheels

If Dallas streets at the turn of the century were paved at all, it was with bois d'arc blocks. Most streets were packed earth, slotted by wagon wheels and perforated by hooves. *Courtesy of DeGolyer Library, Southern Methodist University.*

of early conveyances and perforated by the hooves of the animals that pulled the vehicles. At any time, drivers, their teams and pedestrians could find the streets powdery and cracked (during the dry seasons), rutted and muddy (during wet times) or lined with bumpy ribs (in freezing weather). The uneven surfaces resulted in pedestrians cracking their ankles or falling face-first into the dirt.

Inconsistent surface conditions affected skittish draft animals, too, sending some into uncontrolled flight. In fact, runaway livestock—often with a wheeled vehicle and passengers still attached—was Dallas's first traffic danger.

⸻•⸻

"UNLESS SOMETHING SHOULD BE speedily done to check the dangers," the *Daily Times Herald* wrote about runaways in August 1897, "there would be a boon for undertakers." The intent of the article, an editor added, "is to plead again for the lives of innocent people jeopardized unnecessarily every hour through no fault of their own."[1]

The *Herald*'s ardent editorial resulted from an incident the previous day, when Baley Talbot, a familiar Dallas saloonkeeper, was attempting to sell his carriage horse to a Mr. Fishminger. Fishminger tied his horse to his own buggy and the two men harnessed Talbot's animal. They drove south on Ervay Street to Grand Avenue to see how Talbot's horse performed. As they turned the horse for the return trip, the animal lost its footing in a series of potholes. Frightened, the horse broke into a full-out run toward downtown, taking the buggy and two men with him. Talbot said he and Fishminger put their combined strength to the buggy's reins without slowing the horse a bit. The horse sped across the Santa Fe tracks, and the rails sent the buggy and Mr. Fishminger flying. (Fishminger escaped without injury but later said he thought his time had come.)

Meanwhile, the horse—still pulling the buggy, Talbot and Fishminger's horse—continued its furious run up Ervay Street, careening from one side of the street to the other. Unaware of the commotion, four men were seated on chairs in front of the South Dallas Firehouse. Their chairs were in the street gutter so they could prop their feet on the curbstone. They didn't hear the runaway until it was right on top of them. Two jumped away, but two were run over and dragged into the street.

The crazed horse then took to the sidewalk and struck a telegraph pole, splintering the buggy and throwing Talbot to the ground. It dragged the buggy's wreckage (with Fishminger's horse still attached) six blocks farther, sending pedestrians and other vehicles fleeing before coming to an exhausted halt in the city park.[2]

Newspapers deplored the event, in which "an unmanageable horse, pitched in fearful speed through one of our principal driving avenues, maimed three men, two being seriously injured, with death sitting at the bedside of the third." Both city newspapers called on authorities to act (or at least put the matter under study).[3]

The danger from runaways continued unabated for two more decades, although the city passed an ordinance in 1906, prohibiting horses from standing on the street unattended while not hitched to one of the sidewalk posts installed for that purpose. Police chief R.P. Keith told the public: "I desire to warn the owners of horses that the ordinance will be strictly enforced." (The practice was so commonplace and traffic police were in such short supply that the ordinance continued to be largely ignored.)[4]

———◆———

Those photographs of early Dallas streets dating from before 1890 or so might show a single—very narrow—set of rails running down the middle of the roadway. These were tracks for the mule cars, Dallas's first stab at public transportation. Two stolid mules pulled a lightweight railcar meant for no more than sixteen passengers down the middle of the street at a pace barely faster than a brisk walk. Mule cars—which made their first appearance in Dallas in 1873—provided only a minor disruption to the usual traffic of horsemen, buggies and wagons. They were slow and easy to avoid, and their routes were mostly straight. But when the track made a turn, it did so on a tight radius and with no warning signal. A driver clopping alongside one of the little cars could, if he wasn't paying strict attention, find the car suddenly swerving into him or, even worse, broadside in front of him.[5]

That's what happened to Mike Hurley, a twenty-five-year-old blacksmith with two small children, on August 29, 1892. On his way home from work, Hurley was attempting to board a moving mule car on Harwood Street when it suddenly swerved, knocking him to the ground and under the iron wheels. Both sets of wheels rolled over his pelvis and legs, crushing bones and almost amputating one limb. The driver, who was likely intoxicated, later claimed he was unaware of the accident and continued along his route with no alarm or cry for assistance. Hurley never recovered and died two months later from his injuries.[6]

Some Dallas transit companies began to replace the slow mule cars with the faster "dummies," miniature steam locomotives designed to look like transit cars. The heavier dummies could barge their way through street traffic but had a much longer stopping distance. They first appeared in Dallas in 1888, shortly before the widespread use of electricity. Before being replaced by electric streetcars, however, the dummies were responsible for their own brand of mayhem on Dallas streets.

One of the early dummies—named *Cyclone* for its speed—started its usual morning run at 7:45 a.m., carrying a full load of passengers from Commerce and Austin Streets, south on Lamar Street, toward the Dallas Cotton and Woolen Mills. *Cyclone* engineer Dee Vinnedge liked to put on extra speed along the Lamar stretch in order to beat a morning passenger train to a railroad crossing near the mills. On the morning of April 29, 1889, as *Cyclone* approached the crossing, Vinnedge was either running late or the

Mule cars traveled only as fast as the old mule could be coaxed to walk, but they were a convenient way to get from one end of downtown to the other. *Courtesy of the Dallas Public Library.*

passenger train was running early. Simultaneously, the engineers of the big and little locomotives caught sight of each other, slammed their levers into reverse and fully opened the drive valves. Both engineers bailed out of their cabs. Their quick actions prevented possible derailments and fatalities; the resulting collision was little more than a soft kiss.[7]

As the two engineers stood by the roadbed, brushing themselves off and marveling at their good fortune, Vinnedge saw his little *Cyclone* begin to back up. He sprinted for the cab, but the steam engine—locked in reverse and with the speed valve fully open—outran him. The engineer watched as his unmanned locomotive and panicking passengers rolled faster and faster back down the track, toward town.

As the runaway locomotive continued to accelerate down Lamar Street, astonished pedestrians and drivers could hear its passengers screaming for help. At Austin Street, the speeding car crashed rear-first into a taxi, sending pieces of the carriage, both horses and the driver flying through the intersection.

Finally, at Commerce Street, the *Cyclone* ran out of track. With a crash that sheared off a steel wheel, the *Cyclone* flew off the track at Commerce

The "Cyclone" was a miniature locomotive. Steam-powered streetcars soon disappeared, replaced by electric streetcars. *Courtesy of DeGolyer Library, Southern Methodist University.*

Street and continued rolling along the roadway for a full city block to Main Street. An oversized curbstone finally halted the car and prevented the small locomotive—passengers and all—from crashing through the door of the Cabinet Saloon.

The dummies—faster than the mule cars but unpleasantly loud and extremely dangerous—were retired from Dallas streets after just two years, and from 1892 to 1898, electric streetcars began replacing mule cars. Multiple transit companies competed for business, all of them recognizing that mule cars were too slow for long hauls and that the technology of electric cars wasn't yet living up to its promise.[8]

By 1890, mule car service was running along more than twenty miles of Dallas streets, using 50 cars and 251 mules. But electric cars would come to dominate. Dallas mayor W.C. Connor could brag in 1892: "We have fourteen miles of electric road. No persons or horses have been killed or injured."[9]

A turning electric streetcar demolished the front end of this automobile. This driver was lucky; other drivers died under the steel wheels of the silent ten-ton juggernauts. *Courtesy of Hardin-Simmons University Library.*

But it didn't take long to discover that the new electric streetcars were the biggest traffic hazards yet. The electric cars on Dallas streets weighed more than ten tons (and later cars would weigh twice that). The early electrics could travel at an astounding eight miles an hour, but because they used manual friction brakes, they took more than fifty yards to come to a full stop. The weight, speed and long stopping distance soon made them the most dangerous vehicles on Dallas streets.

———•———

"THE BOY WAS THE victim of one of those modern Juggernauts, an electric car." The newspaper account of Angus Cox's sudden death appeared under the headline, "Boy Mangled and Crushed."[10] In the earliest years of their use, the electric streetcars were particularly lethal to youngsters. It was the summer of 1902, school was out, and nine-year-old Angus and a friend were playing around an ice wagon that was parked in front of a home on Ross Avenue. He might've seen his mother waving from the porch of their residence across the street; the boy turned away from the wagon and ran toward his house. His mother gave out a wild scream and covered her face, a neighbor said. Angus was struck down and dragged twenty-five feet under an electric streetcar. Passersby picked up the little boy and carried him to his house. His right leg had been nearly severed at the hip, and a bone protruded several inches from the flesh. His skull was crushed in two places. Angus died within the hour.

Youngsters like Angus regularly used the streets as playgrounds. Riders and drivers at walking speed could easily rein their animals or swerve to avoid the little nuisances, but the almost silent electric cars moved too fast and braked too slowly to avoid heedless youngsters. (And the "Stop! Look! Listen!" phrase wasn't generally adopted as a safety warning until the early 1920s.) Electric streetcars took a terrible toll on adult pedestrians as well as youngsters at play. But the weight and speed of the cars would also win any contest against buggies or wagons.

Later that same year, fireman Arthur Coffman was driving the department's official buggy as he and Chief H.F Magee rushed to a fire. As the speeding buggy raced down Crowdus Street, Coffman was forced to swing wide around two stopped wagons in order to make the sharp left turn onto Commerce Street. He didn't see the electric streetcar until it was too late. Chief Magee jumped free of buggy, suffering only bruises; Coffman was caught in the crash, and when he was extricated from what was left of the buggy, he was found to be seriously injured. The buggy was reduced to splinters, and a trained fire horse died under the streetcar's wheels.[11]

Electric streetcars were becoming so common on crowded Dallas streets that they were running into each other. One particularly destructive rush hour collision in 1907 cost a young man his life and injured twenty others.[12]

Elmer Geeson was a sixteen-year-old blacksmith's apprentice; he and longtime friend Mark Wilson usually rode home from work on the eastbound Commerce Street streetcar to their homes near Grand Avenue. The boys boarded the car near the courthouse and found seats together. By the time the car crossed St. Paul Street, it was jammed shoulder to shoulder with passengers; the boys gave up their seats to women and took standing spots on the rear platform. It was April 26, the weather was mild and a nice breeze blew through the length of the car. The electric car continued to load passengers, and by the time it stopped at Duncan Street, even the rear platform was jammed tight.

Witnesses said that the first car was still stopped at Duncan Street when a following electric streetcar plowed into the rear of the car. Some passengers saw the streetcar approaching and were able to jump clear; the majority were wedged so tightly in the rear platform that they were compelled to stand and watch in horror as they received the impact. Geeson caught the full force of the blow from the rear car against the front one; his legs were crushed, and the platform rail cut him almost in two at the abdomen. He died later that evening.[13] Twenty others sustained injuries—some life-threatening—in this collision of juggernauts.[14]

The hefty electric streetcars—which would continue to increase in size and weight through the following half-century—may have been juggernauts, but the real behemoths were the passenger and freight trains that rumbled along Dallas streets.

In 1872, the Houston & Texas Central Railroad laid its depot and north–south rail trackbed on the prairie about one mile east of the Dallas Courthouse. Shortly afterward, the (east–west) Texas & Pacific built through Dallas, creating a flourishing city out of the little frontier town. Dallas became a rail crossroads, and soon, other railroad companies announced plans to build lines out of the town in other directions.

The trade-off for this good fortune was that Dallas would grant rights-of-way to the rail companies, allowing them to run track across and along city streets. As the Dallas commercial district expanded to the east, north and south, more streets were affected. There were no crossing gates, flashing lights, wig-wag signs or crossbucks; drivers—including streetcar motormen—had to look both ways at crossings, then proceed at their own risk. Until about 1923, Texas & Pacific track ran down the middle of Pacific Avenue. When drivers saw or heard a train, they had to scurry over to the curb or risk being smashed by a locomotive. Accidents were commonplace.

On October 14, 1899, fifty passengers were jammed into an electric streetcar, returning home from a day at the fair. Motorman C.H. Murray came to the Santa Fe tracks at First Avenue, stopped, sounded his warning gong and looked both ways. Though buildings partially blocked his view of the tracks, he didn't see any moving rail cars or flagmen. Murray then engaged the lever to set his streetcar in motion.[15] His passengers spotted the danger before Murray did: a string of sixteen rail cars propelled by a switch engine was bearing down on them; a man stood atop the foremost railroad car, frantically spinning the brake wheel to slow the train.

Early Dallas traffic shared the streets with large locomotives. This woman is walking along a Pacific Avenue sidewalk, next to a smoky Texas & Pacific train. *Courtesy of DeGolyer Library, Southern Methodist University.*

A witness described the collision: "I saw the streetcar was halfway across the Santa Fe track. The motorman was trying to reverse his power, but before he succeeded in getting the car started back and clear of the track, the freight struck the front platform." The train derailed the streetcar (almost overturning it), sheared off the front platform and bent the front axle double.

"When I saw we would get caught," a passenger said, "I jumped from the car and escaped with only a trifling injury." He was lucky. At least seven passengers were seriously injured, most with broken or crushed bones and spinal injuries. Physicians arrived quickly at the scene and sent seven people to local hospitals and many more to nearby residences to have their wounds dressed. One passenger later died of his injuries, and two were paralyzed for life.

These horrendous collisions continued on downtown streets until tracks were eventually removed from along Pacific Avenue in 1923 and most at-grade crossings were rerouted by the late 1930s.

——•——

AT THE END OF 1899, as the nineteenth century gave way to the twentieth, all manner of vehicles crowded Dallas streets: horses with wary riders dodged teams of oxen pulling loaded freight wagons; smaller delivery carts and wagons jockeyed for curbside access; buggies would veer from one side of the road to the other as shoppers searched for specific businesses; electric streetcars rushed through the traffic, trying to meet schedules; bicyclists filled whatever traffic gaps remained; and freight and passenger trains rode on tracks down and across crowded streets. Pedestrians had to be on high alert and step lively to cross from one side of the street to the other. (Street traffic was so dangerous that the *Dallas Morning News* printed a column calling for underground sidewalks, so at least the pedestrians could navigate in safety.)[16] "Dallas leads all other Texas cities by long odds in the number of its conveyances, both public and private," according to one newspaper. "Everyone has observed the endless procession of buggies, carriages, express wagons, carts, etc., on the main downtown streets."[17]

As bad as traffic conditions were, the new century would bring a new type of vehicle that made the roadways even more crowded and decidedly more dangerous.

At 7:30 p.m. on October 5, 1899, railroad millionaire E.H.R. Green drove the first production automobile into Dallas. He had departed his home in Terrell five hours earlier in a brand-new two-cylinder, water-cooled gasoline buggy.[18] "We didn't put on full power on the country roads because it would have been too dusty for comfort," Green said of his trip to Dallas. "When we struck the asphalt pavement on Main Street, we dared not do so because the thoroughfare was so crowded that it would have been dangerous to human life." Green spent several hours driving the gasoline buggy up and down lighted sections of Main Street and Ross Avenue, squeezing the horn bulb at every opportunity and enjoying himself immensely.[19]

At first, the automobile was a rich man's toy, with an average cost in excess of $1,200. By 1905, an estimated eighty machines were being driven on Dallas city streets. Besides contributing to the problem of overcrowded streets, these new automobiles brought their own particular set of problems.

"Fright from an automobile caused a team of horses hitched to a cab to break away from the place where they were tied, dangerously injuring another horse and doing considerable damage to the vehicle to which they were attached." Automobiles—steam-driven, electric-powered and the "explosives" (internal combustion)—were noisy. The *pop-pop-pop* from gasoline explosions or the roar of steam engines at close quarters frightened otherwise placid draft animals and caused many to bolt. More automobiles meant more runaways and more roadway havoc.[20]

At the beginning of the automobile era, there were as many "learner" drivers on the street as there were automobiles. Otherwise capable men who'd grown up pulling on reins to stop a buggy had some difficulty remembering to use a mechanical foot brake. Virtually every newspaper of the time printed stories of motorists crashing through store display windows while yelling "Whoa!" at their runaway autos.

Methods of mass production soon drove the price of these self-propelled vehicles down to a price affordable to middle-class families. Just ten years after

Automobile ownership made it easier for people who lived outside of Dallas (such as this proud Mesquite couple) to come into the city, further crowding Dallas streets and roads. *Courtesy of Historic Mesquite Inc.*

Green's first motorized carriage chugged into Dallas, Texas had registered more than fourteen thousand personal automobiles; two years later, there were thirty-three thousand.[21]

A four-way accident involving an electric streetcar, a city dump cart, a phaeton carriage and a new automobile typified the chaos on Dallas streets. At Commerce and Martin Streets, the No. 76 eastbound streetcar, while slowing to pick up a passenger, clipped cart No. 55 of the city's street cleaning service. The cart, driven by G.W. Johnson, overturned, coming to rest across the hood of an automobile parked outside the salesroom where proud owner Mr. J.W. Atwood was just then concluding his purchase. The horse that had been pulling the cart righted itself and, after some vicious kicks to the radiator and passenger door, fled westward toward the courthouse, where Mrs. H.L. Marriner was waiting in the carriage for her husband to make a few small purchases in a nearby store. Just as Mr. Marriner exited the store with his three new handkerchiefs, he (simultaneously) heard Mrs. Marriner scream like a banshee, saw the runaway cart horse plow into the rear wheels of his phaeton and steadied his own carriage horse so it would not run away with Mrs. Marriner.[22]

The addition of automobiles didn't mean that people were giving up their four-legged transport. Motorized vehicles would eventually come to own Dallas streets, but for the first twenty years of the twentieth century, automobiles would share Dallas roads with horses, mules and the rigs that they hauled.

———•———

WHEN AUTOMOBILES FIRST APPEARED on Dallas streets, there were no laws to govern them. Drivers felt free to veer from one side of the road to the other to look at store displays—a practice that soon became known as "window shopping"—or greet a friend who might be walking on an opposite sidewalk. Some drivers tried to race fire department vehicles to the scene of a fire. There were no laws requiring lights for night driving, no requirement to signal a change in direction. Even pedestrians were unregulated on city streets. (Dallas Police Court didn't levy its first jaywalking fine until 1914.)[23] But the biggest risk to life and property was speeding. Each year, automobiles became more powerful, and top speeds increased. For a new motorist to show off their top speed or to best their neighbors in an informal auto race was a self-evident brag.

Cabby Dick Alsbrook earned a charge of murder in the death of Edward Hall when he plowed his taxicab into (and over) the young man at 2:00 a.m. on Akard Street, near Ross Avenue. Hall and a friend, who were walking back to their rooming house on Harwood Street, stepped off the curb and into the path of Alsbrook's taxi. A witness said the taxi was running at more than thirty miles an hour without lights. Hall was "knocked for a good distance and run over by the car" before it could stop. Hall never regained consciousness.[24]

Contests of speed were a regular occurrence on Dallas streets, and a particularly popular track for late-night races was South Ervay Street, between Grand Avenue and Main Street. One observer volunteered to be a passenger and was amazed by the speed. "I got into the rig with him," the observer said. "He went so fast, straight away and around curves that I had to hold onto my hat with one hand and the seat of the rig with the other." The passenger estimated that the automobile might have been traveling as fast as fifty miles an hour. "The best way I have of judging is that a dog usually runs after me when I am mounted [and barks]. We left him like he was standing still. It may be that he barked and we outran the sound."[25]

Ervay Street residents announced a mass meeting "to devise ways and means to prevent the dangerous speeding of automobiles on that thoroughfare." They planned to take their concerns to city commissioners and demand relief. The police chief assigned officers on horseback to control traffic, but there was little they could do to halt the recklessness and carelessness.[26]

———◆———

AS CITY COMMISSIONERS STRUGGLED to resolve traffic issues brought on by the addition of automobiles, early automobile owners chartered a new social/civic organization that was determined to bring order to the vehicular chaos on Dallas streets. The Dallas Automobile Association was chartered in July 1904 by sixteen (generally) wealthy owners of some of the first automobiles in the city. They announced their purpose was "to work for better roads and the protection of their machines," but their first activity was to organize a July Fourth parade and road race.[27]

During its long life and many iterations, the Dallas Automobile Association would be a social club, a city booster, a racing promoter, a sales promotion organization and a travel agency. For the first three decades of the twentieth

With few traffic laws and fewer lane markers, drivers were free to veer across both sides of the street for "window shopping." This driver should've been looking straight ahead. *Courtesy of Dallas Public Library.*

century, however, members recognized that, "to share the joy of motoring," it would be necessary to resolve some of the city's traffic issues.

Texas cities, counties and the state legislature passed some laws regulating auto traffic, but the laws were incomplete and, too often, contradictory. (Texas was the last in the nation to establish a state highway department in 1917.) Dallas finally passed a speeding ordinance in 1907, limiting speed on city streets eight miles an hour.[28] But Dallas police chief Robert Cornwell seemed unable to curb speeders. Beat cops were of little use in chasing automobiles on foot, and policemen mounted on horseback created even more danger on Dallas streets. In 1909, the chief assigned a special detail of motorcyclists to curb speeding motorists.

City judge Walter Mathis was also weary of the disregard for the ordinance. He promised to throw the book at speeders, imposing the maximum fine possible. (It was five dollars.)

The Dallas Automobile Association, on the other hand, argued for a comprehensive municipal vehicle ordinance and strict enforcement. It formed committees of study and committees of correspondence to contact other cities for samples of traffic codes and optimum means of enforcement. A blue-ribbon committee—comprised of influential businessmen—presented their plan to municipal commissioners and the public. "At the suggestion of the Dallas Automobile Club, the city is now considering the better regulation of traffic on the streets of Dallas," a newspaper editorial read. "The ordinance submitted by the club represents extensive work and study, and the motorists believe its suggested provisions are wise and needful."[29] The club's draft included fifty-one sections, each prescribing a type of motoring behavior that would become common in the following years: keeping to the right side of the street, yielding to emergency vehicles, showing lights at night, et cetera. Commissioners passed the proposal in 1911, with minor alterations, and much of the language in today's municipal traffic codes still contains wording that originated from the Dallas Automobile Club.[30]

Despite the new laws and the police chief's promises, enforcement lagged. Three fatalities caused by speeders in early 1912—including one involving the death of an eight-year-old girl—brought about public frustration and even rumors of vigilantism. ("Men who had children on that street told me they had loaded shotguns to avenge the murder of any member of their family, as they could not look to the city authorities for protection.")[31]

Delegations from the Dallas Automobile Association continued to visit city commissioners and police officials, and police vowed increased enforcement. Eventually, the general congestion of downtown streets slowed the speeders there, but the jumble of motorized and non-motorized vehicles—along with an increasing number of pedestrians—resulted in all combinations of collisions between streetcars, locomotives, automobiles, motorcycles, carts, wagons, horses and walkers. Street striping, intersection signaling systems and rerouting most train tracks only dampened the number of injuries and fatalities.

The passage of the Volstead Act and the beginning of Prohibition in 1920 brought another, even more egregious type of vehicular offender onto Dallas streets.

———◆———

JESSE HASSELL, PRESIDENT OF the Dallas Steers baseball team, made no secret of the fact that he enjoyed a few beers in the afternoon. A Marine Field maintenance man's father brewed beer in the old-fashioned German way, so Hassell had a ready supply. Prohibition be damned.

Hassell certainly had a few beers on Wednesday afternoon, November 24, 1920, as he was driving one of his employee's home. Witnesses said Hassell was driving east on Commerce Street as he approached Ervay Street and a streetcar that was stopped to discharge passengers. At first, Hassell seemed to brake to avoid the streetcar, then accelerated to swerve along the right side of it. Mrs. S.C. Ham, a mother of three, was stepping off the curb to enter the streetcar when Hassell's car struck her, knocking her ten feet into the intersection. Hassell ran over her before he could stop his car; he then reversed, and the car's wheels ran over Mrs. Ham again. Hassell's passenger pulled Mrs. Ham from under the vehicle, folded her up and put her into the back seat. With Hassell still at the wheel, they zoomed off in search of medical attention, but Mrs. Ham was dead by the time they arrived at St. Paul Hospital.[32]

Police later determined that Hassell was drunk to the point of incoherence, and he was charged with negligent homicide. After pleading guilty and making a payment of $30,000 to Mrs. Ham's children, Hassell was fined $10,000 and released.[33]

America's era of Prohibition had some unforeseen side effects. Adults who were determined to drink illegal alcohol could no longer congregate openly in public bars or saloons. Instead, many chose to drink in the privacy of their automobiles. Arrests for drunken driving surged during the 1920s.[34]

Hassell was not a one-time drunk driver. In February 1921, three months after killing Mrs. Ham, Hassell sideswiped a car on North Marsalis Avenue, injuring two women. Just days after he pled guilty for the death of Mrs. Ham, he drove into a sidewalk construction tunnel in front of the Magnolia Building on Commerce, sozzled again. On November 8, 1921, he was once again arrested for driving while intoxicated and for giving the police a false name. When a drunken Hassell injured two more people, District Judge E.B. Muse was fed up with the stack of drunk driving arrests in the man's file. He ruled that Hassell behind the wheel was a public menace and revoked his driving privileges.[35]

In addition to losing his driver's license, Hassell lost his job, his wife through divorce and his house through seizure by the district attorney. Still, Hassell seemed determined to view Dallas streets through the bottom of a beer mug. Three weeks after being banned from driving, Hassell was again arrested for drunk driving when he collided with the car of an older couple on their way to church. The court threw the book at Hassell, sentencing him to two years in jail and a $1,000 fine. (The sentence was later reduced, and Hassell did no time.)[36]

Dallas suffered an epidemic of alcohol-related accidents during the 1920s, but those incidents were lost in an ever-increasing number of accidents and infractions by drivers of automobiles. In 1925, half of the city's thirty-six thousand docketed court cases were automobile related.[37]

Non-motorized vehicles—the carts, buggies and wagons—were mostly gone from downtown Dallas streets by the end of the 1920s. But the increasing size and speed of American automobiles ensured that horrendous (and deadly) crashes would continue to occur. In just the first ten months of 1930, when 65 people were killed on Dallas streets in motor vehicle accidents, it was the nation's highest death toll among cities of 100,000 to 300,000.[38]

Traffic congestion and the number of traffic deaths in Dallas would increase for the next ninety years, but as a percentage of urban street miles and vehicles, no period was as deadly on Dallas streets as the turn of the twentieth century.

DEADLY DALLAS WEATHER

Twenty-six-year-old May Johnson and her two sons lived in a one-room sled cabin on the Widow Bass Farm in the outskirts of Hutchins. May cooked and did chores for Mrs. Bass in return for the use of the cabin. What little cash she earned came from taking in sewing from time to time and selling whatever fish the boys could catch in the Trinity River. The cabin had no kitchen and no indoor plumbing; a ladder-back chair and a rope bed were the only furnishings. A small wood stove in one corner provided the heat.[39]

The winter had not been a harsh one, but the cabin was always cold at night. May had chinked most of the gaps with old newspapers and scrounged whatever firewood she could gather. May and her boys, five and eight years old, slept huddled together under a single blanket on most winter nights.

By mid-March 1896, it seemed that winter was gone. Nights still held a bit of winter's chill, but days were bright and sunny, with temperatures reaching into the low seventies, according to the thermometer outside Mrs. Bass's kitchen door. March 17 was one of those temperate days, but the air felt denser, humid—as if there might be a rain shower on the way. While walking back to her cabin that evening, May saw a line of low blue-black clouds with anvil tops stretched across the northern horizon.

The Texas blue norther rolled over the Red River, across North Texas and through Dallas County, arriving in Hutchins just before sundown. The sky turned black as a mourner's bonnet, and a frigid wind built up from the north. The blast of arctic air was a wedge at its front, slicing under the ground layer of warm, moist Gulf air, lifting it thousands of feet upward, where it froze and fell as hail and sleet. In three hours, Dallas County temperatures fell forty-seven degrees Fahrenheit. In rural areas, the overnight low temperature was a wet, bitter twenty-two degrees Fahrenheit.

May wasn't prepared for this unexpected return of ice and bitter cold. She had no warm food for the boys; there was no firewood for the stove. Even the kindling box was empty but for a few sticks. To beg shelter from Widow Bass would be hopeless.

Sometime during the night, May dressed her boys in every piece of clothing they owned and told them they would go to stay with relatives in Oak Cliff when the sun came up. The three of them spent the night shivering under a single blanket on the rope bed. Perhaps they prayed.

At an early hour the next morning, the two boys came to the door of H.C. Keithley, who lived nearby. The boys told him they "were dressed up and were going to Oak Cliff." Keithley asked, "Where is your mother?" The older boy replied that she had frozen to death during the night. The little boys had spent the dismal night shivering under the same rough blanket that covered their mother's corpse.

———•———

DALLAS RARELY EXPERIENCES THE days-long blizzards that are more common in the Midwestern states; it settles, instead, for an every-other-year-or-so day of snow and ice. A century ago, as today, snow and ice days in Dallas were most often celebration days of snowmen and sledding.

But Texas blue northers could be killers.

Blue northers—which usually occur from November through April—arrive unannounced. At the turn of the twentieth century, an early warning might consist of a telegraphic notice from a station to the north, warning of sudden drops in temperature and a fast-rising barometer reading. But many didn't know of the danger until the hail, rain, wind and bitter cold were upon them. The homeless, impaired and rural folk were the most vulnerable.

Amos Christian had been released from the Dallas jail in early March 1882 and was walking to Terrell. He traveled only a few miles before a late-season norther blew through. Christian became disoriented in the rain and darkness, eventually stumbling across a farmhouse outside Forney. The farmer turned him away but gave him directions to a church where he might seek refuge. His body was found the next day, rigid with cold and death.

"It seemed he had attempted to crawl through a wire fence," a newspaper reported. "His clothing became tangled in the barbs, and he did not have strength enough to extricate himself."[40]

Another norther took the life of L.C. McDonald in 1912. McDonald, forty-five, lived under the care of his father on Second Street. He was known to many in the city for his habit of meeting trains at the Katy station and welcoming arriving passengers to Dallas with a beaming smile and a friendly wave. On the night of January 6, as his father slept and the temperature dropped to below freezing, MacDonald left his home and set out for the station. The next morning, arriving passengers found him on the ground behind the station. He was wearing two suits of underwear, two pairs of trousers, two coats, a sweater, a heavy top shirt, an overcoat and mismatched all-weather overshoes. Despite the clothing, he froze to death, waiting for a train that never arrived.[41]

Even if a farm family didn't lose their lives, a surprise Texas blue norther could cost them their livelihood. The unexpected drop in temperature could kill unprotected livestock in the fields; hailstones could wipe out a farm wife's flock of chickens, the birds too stupid to seek shelter in the coop. And the combination of heavy wind, driving rain and bitter cold could wipe out a valuable crop of cotton or wheat in a few hours.

A LONG-AGO TEXAS HUMORIST often told the story of his grandfather, who had an old Native American as a tenant on his farm. One day, the grandfather rode out to see his tenant. Standing on the property, the two men heard an owl hoot three times.[42] The Native American said, "Owl calls three times, means winter over, good weather ahead." Two weeks later, after a continuing parade of thunderstorms and cold fronts, the grandfather again rode out to see his tenant.

"You sure were wrong about that owl," the grandfather said.

"Young owl. Damned fool."

This old story illustrates an even earlier saying: "No one but fools and newcomers try to forecast Texas weather." The saying was especially true at the turn of the twentieth century.

Before the telegraph was in wide use, information about weather in other regions could travel no faster than a horse. News of current weather elsewhere could be useful in wartime, and during the Civil War, telegraphy

Gustave Eisenlohr was a volunteer who collected daily readings of temperature, precipitation and barometric pressure for twenty-three years from his cousin's drugstore. *Courtesy of the Dallas Public Library.*

companies began collecting weather data and sharing it via wire. However, there was no organized effort to use the data to predict future weather.[43]

President Ulysses S Grant, in 1870, signed a bill requiring the secretary of war to provide for taking standardized meteorological observations "for giving notice on the northern lakes and on the seacoasts…on the approach and force of storms." This act marked the beginning of a national weather service as part of the U.S. Army Signal Service.

In 1890, weather collection duties were handed off to a newly created civilian agency, the U.S. Weather Bureau in the Department of Agriculture. Its function was still primarily data collection and reporting. The bureau started issuing flood warnings when it began to collect flow data from observation stations along the Mississippi River and its major tributaries.

Despite the volume of past weather information that had been collected, prediction seemed an almost impossible task. However, some private companies marketed long-range weather predictions in the form of almanacs or syndicated newspaper columns. Their predictions were often guesses, no more accurate than a savvy farmer might make with his own thermometer and barometer.[44]

The lack of accurate short-term forecasts prevented farmers from knowing what and when to plant or harvest; municipalities couldn't prepare their cities for flood, drought or blizzards; and devasting storms could tear through populated areas without warning.

An unexpected hurricane struck Galveston in September 1900, resulting in what is still the deadliest natural disaster in American history. Weather bureau observers recognized that a storm was building in the Gulf of Mexico, but they had little way of tracking its location, timing or direction of travel. The hurricane made landfall at Galveston Island, where wind and flooding took the lives of six thousand people.[45]

Dallas had little to fear from surprise hurricanes, but cyclones were another matter.

———•———

CYCLONES ARE DESTRUCTIVE SPIRALING storms—usually accompanied by heavy rain—comprised of strong winds rotating around a center of low pressure. Because the center of the storm covers a larger area, the cyclone's winds are usually not as high as a tornado and are often more localized. Even so, a cyclone is perfectly capable of tearing a farmhouse into splinters or toppling mature trees. And at the turn of the century, a cyclone usually arrived without warning.

Gus Spencer and several friends were building an addition to his farmhouse in southeast Dallas County on a hot August afternoon in 1907. A sudden rainstorm at about 4:00 p.m. forced the men indoors from the porch they were framing. "In a twinkling of an eye," Spencer said, "a cyclone tore the house to pieces."[46] Spencer jumped out a window and escaped the collapse without a scratch. His helpers suffered painful injuries from falling timbers. By the time Spencer pulled the men from the wreckage, the sky was bright and clear.

A 1903 cyclone collapsed the school building in Seagoville, injuring four students there. Eighteen months later, a cyclone took the roof off the Western Union Telegraph Company's building in Dallas, allowing rain to short out most of the equipment and cut off communication with the rest of the world.[47]

In most cases, a cyclone's damage is limited to several city blocks, and the destruction is usually caused by blowing, rather than lifting, winds. Tornadoes, on the other hand, rotate around a smaller core, meaning that wind speeds far exceed those of cyclones. Though newspapers called it a cyclone at the time, the storm that sliced through a sleeping Dallas County in the predawn hours of January 20, 1894, was most likely a full-fledged tornado.

———◆———

THE MOON AND STARS shone in a crystal-clear sky at bedtime on January 19. The day's temperature had been spring-like, and a gentle wind hardly stirred the bare trees. A light sleeper may have noticed the wind picking up at midnight, an easterly wind just strong enough to cause the same tree branches to tap against windows but not strong enough to raise concern. During the early hours of the morning, the wind shifted direction, first from the north, then east again and then south.[48]

The storm struck at 2:00 in the morning.

Bomb-like booms of thunder woke children and drove men and women out of their beds and onto porches. Lightning illuminated low black clouds. "The whole heavens were sheets of flashing fire," one observer said. The whirlwind entered Oak Cliff from the southwest, touching down on Ninth Street and filling the air with debris from toppled fences and demolished outbuildings. At Ninth and Beckley Streets, the storm pulled First Christian Church from its foundation and dropped it on its side, shattering the framework. W.J. Parchman's home on Eighth Street was blown from its foundation; the occupants rushed from the house, dodging bricks falling from a ruined chimney.

As the storm moved eastward, the bell in the steeple of Oak Cliff Methodist Church began to toll, rocked back and forth by the force of the wind. The church wasn't spared. The wind tore the steeple away, ending the mournful tolling of the church bell that many heard over the roar of the storm. Near the church, Frank Johnson watched the wind flatten his home and explode his henhouse, sending poultry flying. One of his roosters was blown ten feet against a barn wall, where a sharp hook protruded. The rooster hung, impaled on the hook and featherless.

The storm turned northeast toward Dallas, leaving a trail of homes without roofs, flattened fences and amputated chimneys. As the tornado crossed the Trinity Bottoms, some later said they could hear big elm trees on the riverbanks splashing into the water as they toppled. Bois d'arc trees were ripped up by the wind; branches and roots added to the debris swirling overheard.

In South Dallas, a smokestack on the powerhouse of the transit company collapsed onto several cars, damaging them beyond use. The elegant homes of Gerard Dreyfus and Jacob Rothschild were decapitated, and other homes in the same Akard Street neighborhood suffered severe damage. Continuing

The best protection from a cyclone came from dugout storm shelters like this one. A family who huddled in this shelter survived a storm that toppled trees and demolished their house. *Courtesy of the Clay County Historical Society.*

northeastward, the storm crossed City Park, felling old trees and an electric light tower. Wind blew the windows out of the brick Houston & Texas Central Railroad roundhouse and dislodged its heavy turntable.

For a time, the storm's path turned northward, along Harwood Street, tearing the St. Patrick Catholic Church from its foundation and twisting the building ninety degrees. Frame buildings along Wood and Young Streets were destroyed, wooden awnings were sent flying and heavy curbstones were moved into the streets. The storm was leaving a five-hundred-foot-wide path of destruction as it crossed Central Avenue. When it veered eastward again into East Dallas, it became more powerful still.

Nothing withstood the wind as the funnel drove up Main Street. Homes and businesses on Elm and Commerce were blown into kindling as well. In his house at Main and Duncan Streets, J.T. Mixter awoke to see the walls swaying back and forth like a snake charmer. Before he could wake his wife, the walls blew outward, and the roof fell on both of them, pinning them in their bed. The couple managed to extricate themselves from the fallen beams and joints, and Mixter crawled over the rubble to locate his two boys. He found both of their bodies under some heavy timber. Six-year-old Roy Seets, a recent adoptee, was obviously dead, his head crushed flat by a ceiling beam. Underneath Roy was twelve-year-old Andy Mixter, who was suffocating from the weight of the debris crushing him. Even after his father pulled him from the wreckage, the boy still gasped, trying to draw air into his lungs despite a crushed chest.

Next door to the Mixters, Robert Scott awakened in time to run toward the sleeping rooms of his six children, all girls. Just as he entered the room, the walls buckled, and the ceiling collapsed. With the help of a door frame, Scott managed to support the weight of the collapsed roof on his back as the girls crawled to safety. Scott suffered a broken back and numerous puncture wounds from splinters.

On Elm Street, W.A. Babcock's house literally disappeared from around him, leaving the proprietor of Dallas Coffee and Spice Mills on his bed in the open air. Nearby, the blacksmith shop of Joseph E. Beeman was wrecked. His heavy metal tools and anvils were scattered around the street and on adjacent properties. Farther up Main Street, two widows were trapped in their house by debris blocking the windows and door. The women cried out for help all night but weren't rescued until the morning's light.

The storm destroyed a sizeable portion of the Munger Gin Factory at Elm and Prospect, sending sections of its sheet-iron roof knifing through the neighborhood. A cotton gin and lumber year were reduced to rubble. Three freight cars near Munger's were derailed and left with their roofs twisted off.

Taking a slightly northern turn, the tornado traveled up Crutcher Street, twisting homes off their foundations and wreaking devastation along Worth and Simpson Streets. At the Strother home on Worth Street, a piece of scantling wood struck the house endwise, spearing through the wall, lath and plaster to end up half in and half out of the structure.

As the storm entered the White Rock Creek Bottoms, it was running out of strength, and its path of destruction was narrowing. Some farmhouses reported blown-over fences and outbuildings, but few were damaged as entirely as those in residential Dallas and Oak Cliff.

"That so many homes should be wrecked at such an hour, when all the world—except newspaper people and policemen—are supposed to be asleep is little short of marvelous," the *Dallas Morning News* wrote. The storm had traveled seven miles in under twenty minutes, too far and too fast for any meaningful alarm to be raised. Hundreds suffered injuries, mostly minor cuts and contusions. Early property damage estimates were more than $200,000.

But there was only one fatality.

A funeral was held for six-year-old Roy Seets the following day at the Nettie Methodist Church by his adoptive family. The biological father, who had given his little boy up for adoption four years before, took the child's body back to Elam, where he was laid to sleep alongside his mother.

Tornadoes are not uncommon in North Central Texas, but Dallas was largely spared the fatalities suffered by other communities around the turn of the twentieth century. Nevertheless, there were plenty of other types of weather events capable of killing.

———•———

"WITHIN THE LAST THIRTY-SIX hours, Dallas has been treated to a sample of every variety of weather in the repertoire of the weather bureau," the *Dallas Morning News* noted on November 17, 1902. Two days earlier, the winter weather had been balmy, "bearing that soft tone which suggests violets and marble games." Before sunset, the day turned overcast, shading off into a torrential downpour of rain. Soon, sewers were flooded, basements swamped, streets turned to rivers, and "timer-worn wooden paving blocks floated like corks on the muddy torrents." Before umbrellas had a chance to dry on porches, the weather changed again, and "winds as of March swept through the streets, rattling gray branches and sweeping damp leaves into windows." The wind died down, and the temperature dropped to near freezing, "the cold weather chilling to the backbone and biting in quality."[49] Poetic, to be sure, but such weather extremes in Dallas were hardly unknown. During the years surrounding the turn of the twentieth century, however, those rapid shifts were more likely to result in death for the unprepared.

———•———

OVERNIGHT SNOWFALL IN DALLAS was then, as now, a rare enough occurrence to be enjoyable to most. "Old and young people, rich and poor, all enjoying,

A snow and ice day could be a rare treat for some in Dallas. Others found that the lack of footing and frozen streets meant broken backs and amputated limbs. *Courtesy of the Dallas Public Library.*

some for the first time in their lives, the bliss of coasting down ice-clad hills or sleighing over icy roadways," said one reporter of an overnight snowfall in 1905.[50]

A lengthy cold spell included three inches of snow falling on Valentine's Day in 1895. After nearly a week of ice on the roadways, the snowfall made it easier for people to leave their homes—boots had better traction in the snow, and horses were less likely to slip on the ice. A newspaper reporter observed that the snow didn't "restrain the ladies from coming downtown and getting a supply of valentines.... [There will] be extra work today for the postal clerks," he wrote.[51]

There were accidents, of course. Some shoppers found themselves flat on their backs on the sidewalks due to an uncovered patch of ice. Mrs. Samuel Carruthers was sweeping the snow off the front porch of her Wood Street residence when she slipped and fell, breaking her arm. Charles Schaberle was walking home at midnight from his job at the transit company when he slipped on ice and broke his right leg in two places, both compound fractures. The leg had to be amputated below the knee.

But the most considerable distress was felt by the city's poor. "Applicants yesterday for clothing were more numerous than I have ever seen in the city in any past year," said L.D. Busbee, the executive director of the charity bureau. "It is absolutely distressing to see the dear little children who are brought to the office by their mothers mutely appealing with bare feet and half-naked bodies for the clothing we cannot supply." Busbee appealed to newspaper readers for donations of warm clothing.

One of the heaviest snowfalls in the early decades of the twentieth century fell on Dallas during the second week of February 1910.[52] Six inches of snow on the level and drifts of up to four feet stopped the city in its tracks. Hundreds of men and women walked miles to work because streetcar service was crippled by the snow and ice. Automobiles couldn't navigate the drifts, and even horse-drawn vehicles were bogged down. The poor—with substandard housing, little heavy clothing, low food reserves and no money for coal—once again bore the brunt of the extreme weather. The Salvation Army Headquarters on Bryan Street, near Pacific Avenue, was overrun by those seeking shelter, food and warm clothing. Families huddled with each other for warmth as they waited in line for assistance in temperatures that warmed to only thirteen degrees Fahrenheit during the day.

———•———

AT THE OTHER END of the thermometer is the smothering Dallas heat.

It's an exceptional summer in Dallas when the thermometer doesn't reach one hundred degrees Fahrenheit two or three times. Today, most of us can retreat to air-conditioned homes, offices, stores, theaters or cars to escape the heat. But there was no air-conditioning at the turn of the twentieth century—no electric fans. And life then required more physical labor—often outdoors—regardless of the temperature.

The last week of July 1876 had been scorching; thermometers reached 100 degrees Fahrenheit each day for five consecutive days. On Sunday morning, July 30, the mercury was up to 105 degrees Fahrenheit by the time church sermons ended and worshippers went home for Sunday dinner. Dinner involved lighting and cooking over a wood-burning stove. Even with windows open to catch a stray breeze, there was no relief from the heat.[53] Meanwhile, the temperature continued to rise. Thermometers read 110 degrees Fahrenheit by 2:00 p.m. By 4:00 p.m., it was 114 degrees Fahrenheit, and the dying had begun.

The day was particularly busy at the Crutchfield House. Clerk David L. Williams had registered guests, fetched hacks, run errands and toted luggage up and down two flights of stairs. Overheated, he went to his room for a quick nap. He was found unconscious and died that evening of heatstroke. Nat Hogan, who was visiting Dallas from St. Louis, was unused to the prolonged Texas heat. He died of sunstroke that afternoon at 4:00 p.m. James Burke, a day laborer, worked on Sunday as a loader to earn extra money for his family. He returned home at the end of the day and was found dead by his daughter, who went to wake him—sunstroke.

"In addition to several cases [of sunstroke] which were fatal," the *Dallas Herald* reported, "many occurred in which the extreme heat entirely prostrated and exhausted persons." Agricultural workers on the farms surrounding Dallas were particularly susceptible to overheating. John Brashear was a Confederate veteran from Tennessee who had trouble finding his place in life after the war ended. For thirty years, he drank and drifted, finding odd jobs here and there. When he was sober, Brashear was an eager worker, and he remained sober for the three months he worked on the Martin farm a mile north of the Dallas fairgrounds.[54]

On the morning of July 20, 1892, Martin sent him out in the field on a hay rake while the rest of the family handled oats at the other end of the farm. The day was blistering hot, and when Brashear came back to the

Dallas faced a critical water shortage during the drought of 1909–11. The city sent tank trucks into neighborhoods, allowing residents only a single tub of fresh water daily. *Courtesy of the Dallas Public Library.*

farmhouse for the midday meal, Martin urged him to rest that afternoon. Brashear insisted on returning to the field to finish the job. That evening, when Brashear hadn't returned, Martin and his brother rode out to the field to find him. They found him seated on the hay rake, red-faced and quite dead. A doctor stated that Brashear had died of sunstroke.

Nothing would change summer temperatures in Dallas, but electric fans, evaporative cooling, better building design and the introduction of rudimentary air-conditioning systems would reduce—but not eliminate—the annual death toll due to heatstroke by the 1920s.

————◆————

DALLAS'S GENERALLY FLAT LANDSCAPE exposes it to weather fronts sweeping southeastward from Colorado and the Panhandle, as well as moist air fronts rising from the Gulf of Mexico. When those fronts meet over Dallas, powerful—and deadly—thunderstorms can blossom over the city in minutes.

After a hot, humid morning on August 3, 1914, a thunderstorm struck at noon, blackening the skies and bringing a driving rain, high gusty winds and continual lightning.[55] T.H. Massey was making deliveries in South Dallas when the storm hit. He sought refuge in the offices of the Lagow Sandpit Company, staking his horses outside. When the company's grain building collapsed on his team, Massey rushed out to extricate them. A shed blew over on Massey, breaking his leg. A portion of the roof was blown from the warehouse of the Dallas cotton mill and onto a neighbor's house, wrecking the house and allowing the rain to ruin the inventory stored in the warehouse. The wind blew down two of the large smokestacks at the Armstrong Packing Company and tore out a dozen windows on one side of the building, injuring employees with flying glass. Ten construction workers suffered severe injuries when the house in Oak Cliff they had been building collapsed after being struck by lightning.

The one fatality of the storm was also brought about by lightning. Bob Hill, a teamster, had taken refuge in a tent near the Trinity Gravel Pit west of Dallas off Fishtrap Road. During a break in the rain, he started off to a nearby residence for a drink of water. Close to the house was a low-hanging wire clothesline. He picked it up to pass beneath just as a bolt of lightning struck the tree, running down the wire and into Hill's body. Witnesses saw lightning dance around Hill's body before he could release the wire. He fell to the ground, dead.

——◆——

DALLAS WEATHER HASN'T CHANGED appreciably in the last century, but our awareness of it, indoor lifestyles, ability to better forecast it and systems of alarm have. Dallas's weather remains just as deadly for the unaware and unprepared.

DEADLY DALLAS EXPLOSIONS

What can you expect when anyone can buy dynamite by the crate at the local hardware store; when unregulated steam boilers chug away at most every major construction and drilling site in town; or when natural gas is pumped through uninspected plumbing into Dallas homes and businesses?

Ka-BOOM! (That's what you can expect.)

In turn-of-the-century Dallas, explosions were popping off like the Fourth of July. There were the smaller, more personal explosions that might cost a person his hands or life. And there were the large building-flattening ones that rocked the city to its limestone footings.

From the 1880s through much of the 1920s, Dallas was growing, and technology was changing. There were stumps to be cleared from developing land, and workers found the new nitroglycerine-based dynamite more effective than black powder. Highly flammable natural gas piped into lighting fixtures was replacing kerosene lamps. The increasing availability of gasoline for motorcars encouraged all manner of businesses to adopt it as a solvent. And equipment manufacturers were attaching steam boilers to construction equipment while experimenting with pressure vessels made of steel instead of more expensive iron.

The result? *Ka-BOOM!*

But emerging technologies, the city's growth and increasing urbanization weren't the only reasons for this explosive period in Dallas history. In fact, one of the most horrifying explosive devices had been in everyday use since the earliest families settled along the Trinity River.

———•———

BATES TOMLINSON, A FARMER living just east of Dallas, woke at midnight to give his sick son some medicine. Probably still half-asleep, Tomlinson lit an oil lamp. When the lamp began to sputter and flare, Tomlinson ran for the door to throw it outside. But he was too late. The lamp exploded in his hand, scattering burning oil over his arms and body. Tomlinson died in terrible pain just after noon the following day. He left a wife and nine children.[56]

Humans have used oil lamps for thousands of years to light the nighttime. The earliest were open seashells or clay cups filled with fat or the oils of crushed plants. A wick soaked in the fuel and would burn, providing a flickering light. By 1899, most oil lamps were engineered to burn brighter and longer. Household lamps of the time consisted of two connected compartments: an oil reservoir below and a glass bulb above. A wick—usually braided or tightly woven fabric—connected the two. The wick, saturated with flammable oil in the lower reservoir, draws the oil to the top of the wick in the bulb. There, the oil evaporated into a combustible gas. When the wick was lit, the flammable gas burned with a bright flame, diffused by the glass bulb to provide a flickering light. It was nice light, but it was dangerous. Blow on the wick to extinguish the light, and you might drive the flame down into the oil reservoir, igniting it. Let the fuel reservoir get too low, and the flame could burn its way down the wick into the almost-empty reservoir, igniting the remaining fuel and the volatile gas that has collected there. In either case, the lamp is likely to explode, splashing anyone and anything nearby with flaming oil.

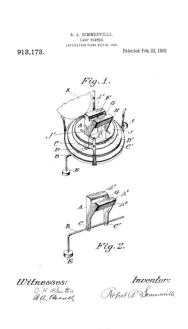

In 1909, a Texas inventor was granted a patent for a lamp burner attachment that automatically extinguished the flame of a lamp if it was tilted. No lampmaker adopted it. *Courtesy of the University of North Texas, Special Collections.*

While visiting friends in Dallas, Mrs. Annie B. Farnham, a Houston resident, and her eight-year-old son, Bobby, stayed in a boardinghouse at 438 Pacific Avenue.

This couple is just one errant elbow away from a fiery death. If the oil lamp should fall to the floor, it would likely shatter and splash fiery oil over the couple and their wooden interior walls. *Courtesy of the University of North Texas, Special Collections.*

Other residents later said Mrs. Farnham was in the habit of keeping an oil lamp burning on a table outside her room to light the way to a bathroom down the hall.[57] No one saw the lamp outside of Mrs. Farnham's bedroom explode at 2:00 a.m. on Saturday morning, July 29, 1899; most boarders were awakened by the crackle, whoosh and hiss of the fire as it set wallpaper ablaze and flared across ceilings to burn upward to the second story. Escaping down burning hallways or through windows, boarders gathered on the street in various states of nightdress to watch flames engulf the entire Pacific Avenue residence.

A quick census of the survivors noted the absence of the Farnham mother and son. Even as the ruined building still smoldered, firemen discovered the still-smoking remains of Mrs. Annie B. Farnham and Bobby. Both were burned beyond recognition, lying just two feet apart. Fire Chief Magee later speculated that Mrs. Farnham allowed the hallway lamp to run low on fuel, and the fiery explosion trapped her and the boy in their room.[58] Two days later, mother and son were buried side by side in white coffins in Greenwood Cemetery.

Exploding oil lamps claimed lives and property at a fearsome rate through the first two decades of the twentieth century. Though gas and electrical lighting were introduced in Dallas in the 1880s, half of Dallas County homes still depended on oil lamps as late as 1925.

———•———

ALFRED NOBEL INVENTED DYNAMITE in the 1860s as a more stable, more powerful alternative to black powder and nitroglycerine. By the 1880s, the eight-inch-long, red paper–wrapped cylinders were as common on farms and at construction sites as hay rakes and claw hammers. Generally, there were no restrictions on purchase. Feed and hardware stores kept dynamite in stock for sale to farmers, who used it to blow stumps, blast out honey pits or demolish unused outbuildings.

Well diggers depended on dynamite when a water well went down more than twenty feet. A helper with an auger would be lowered down the well, where he would dig several holes, plant the dynamite, light the fuse and then signal his boss to pull him to the surface as the fuse burned down.

Well digger John Hammontree was blasting through rock to reach water on the Nelson farm, just south of Oak Cliff, when he lit the dynamite fuses and grabbed a rope that would pull him out of the shaft. Somewhere near the opening, he lost his grip and fell thirty feet to the smoldering explosives. Too injured to hold the rope or reach the burning fuses, Hammontree recited Bible verses until—*ka-BOOM!*

Something similar happened to an amateur Oklahoma well digger in 1904. He fell back into the well, but the charge exploded before he hit bottom. The blast shot him out of the hole and into the air like a champagne cork. The actual explosion didn't hurt him, but he suffered severe injuries when he hit the ground.[59]

Many homeowners kept a few sticks of dynamite in their storage sheds or under their back steps. They dropped it down rat holes to rid themselves of rodent nests, they used it to collapse the dirt under unneeded outhouses and some used it for fishing. (A Van Zandt County man was fishing from a small boat on the Trinity River when he lit the waterproof fuse on a stick of dynamite and threw it overboard, intending to stun the fish and bring them to the surface. Instead of sinking, the dynamite continued to float next to the boat, and the man spent his last few seconds trying to paddle away. *Ka-BOOM!* "He was blown to atoms," the morning newspaper reported.[60]

Most young boys knew where the dynamite was stored in their neighborhoods. For some of them, the temptation was too great.

Nine-year-old Robert Arnett found a stick of dynamite in his father's tool shed. The boy put it into a tin talcum powder box and shook it to make it rattle against the sides of the can. He ended the day in Baptist Sanitarium with doctors trying desperately to save his sight.[61]

The volatile component of dynamite is nitroglycerine. This highly unstable liquid is slowly combined with an absorbent—sawdust, wood pulp and clay are the most common—and rolled into a cylinder, which is then wrapped in a waxed paper. When handled and stored correctly, a stick of dynamite is relatively stable. To explode, dynamite usually requires a cap, a firecracker-like charge made of a fulminating powder, ignited by a burning fuse, an electrical charge or a sharp impact.

Charles Barnes and Leon Young were still teenagers, just boys playing outdoors on a chilly February afternoon in 1909. A nearby neighbor noticed the boys standing face to face in the backyard of the Young's Eagle Ford Roadhouse. One of the boys bent to pick up a box—which police later

You can buy dynamite by the stick or crate at the local hardware store. Have a large order? There's plenty in inventory in this powder company's three storage facilities. *Author's collection.*

determined contained a dozen blasting caps—and the other grabbed for it, causing it to fall to the ground.

Ka-BOOM!

The witness described a brilliant white flash and the sight of the boys being blown fifteen feet in the air. The earth trembled, she said, knocking out glass and rattling doors for some distance around.

The first parties at the scene saw a gruesome sight. The Barnes boy was terribly maimed and obviously dead. Leon Young was still alive, sitting upright on his torso, both legs blown entirely away, his face and chest a crackly char. Still, Young spent his final minutes calling for his mother and father as a neighbor held what was left of his hand.[62]

Working with dynamite is work best left to professionals, but even professionals make mistakes. And all it takes is one mistake.

A well-meaning mistake was all it took for three experienced explosives handlers to set off the largest dynamite explosion in Dallas history. In 1903, the blasting crew from Texas Portland Cement Company set out to dispose of six crates of dynamite "duds." Three hundred pounds of dynamite in storage froze the previous winter and was no longer reliable. They transported the containers of duds to an inactive quarry, placing the first box fifty yards from the others. The blasters wedged a fresh stick of dynamite under the first crate and laid a fuse to a protected area some distance away. At 6:00 a.m., they lit the fuse.

Ka-BOOM!

The blast was strong enough to lift the crew off the ground as the first box—reliably explosive, after all—set off the other five with "a noise that sounded like a blast from the infernal region." The explosion sent a tremor ("not unlike an earthquake shock") across Dallas County.[63] West Dallas residents ran from their homes as windowpanes fractured and crockery fell to the floor. Waking from a dead sleep, an Oak Cliff man in his nightwear ran from his house thinking his chimney was collapsing. A county clerk was milking his cow in the East Dallas suburbs when a usually docile bossie kicked over the bucket (and the clerk) in a scramble to run out of the barn. Fortunately, there were no serious injuries or fatalities.

———◆———

B.R. BOURLAND WAS JUST the sort of up-and-comer Dallas needed in 1914. Still in his thirties, Bourland's reputation as a skilled and hardworking concrete contractor in Dallas was blossoming. He and his wife had moved to the city just a year earlier to take advantage of the building boom, and he immediately won two large contracts with developers. At the time, he was working on his biggest deal yet: a $25,000 project laying the sidewalks and curbs of a new Lakewood addition, Junius Heights, three miles northeast of Dallas.

At dinnertime on April 6, 1914, Bourland told his wife he had completed clearing the land and was eager to build his forms and start laying concrete. Mrs. Bourland was relieved; her husband had spent much of the previous month using dynamite to blast out stumps of old-growth elms and oaks from hard-baked black dirt. He had encountered no particular problems when blasting out one hundred acres of stumps, but his wife was pleased that that part of the job was completed.

The next morning, he set out for work with his tools, but first, he had to return the leftover dynamite and blasting caps to the storage shed. He bent over a wooden crate containing the explosives and—*ka-BOOM!* By the time other workers reached the site, pieces of Bourland were spread in all directions of the compass, some as far as one hundred feet away from the still-smoldering crater. Coworkers speculated that when Bourland bent to pick up the crate of explosives, a metal tool slipped out of an overall pocket and into the box, a tool heavy enough to detonate one of the caps, which caused the sticks to blow the contractor all over the newly platted neighborhood.[64]

———————•———————

LATER IN THE CENTURY, dynamite would become the enforcer of choice for Dallas gangsters and racial fanatics. However, the city apparently experienced its own brand of dynamite terrorism early in the twentieth century.

On December 28, 1909, police in Dallas received word that a dynamite explosion blew out a section of the interurban's track on Greenville Avenue shortly before Texas Traction Company cars would've passed over it. There was nothing to investigate; interurban crews repaired the damage before police could arrive. It was an attempt to stop the train and rob the passengers, police concluded—an effort that was foiled by a premature explosion.[65] Two months later, on March 1, an alert motorman stopped his interurban cars just south of Plano when he noticed a broken rail ahead. Again, a rail was blown out of place by dynamite, and again, police were notified too late to investigate.[66]

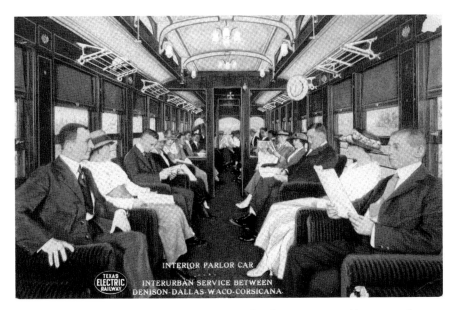

Passengers deserted the interurban cars in droves after there were several instances of dynamite being placed on the tracks. No culprit was found, and the passengers eventually returned. *Courtesy of DeGolyer Library, Southern Methodist University.*

"Dynamite on Track Again," newspaper headlines announced a week later. "Third Mysterious Explosion on Interurban." A new explosive package, this time, set to blow both rails, was discovered near Delmar Heights by security officers hired to walk the track. "Who is this mysterious enemy of the Texas Traction Company?" editorials asked. Police had no answer, and company officials remained mum. With no clues, the Dallas chief of detectives was forced to instruct his detectives to "sweep the town for every suspicious man." Meanwhile, ridership plummeted.[67]

On April 20, another explosion destroyed interurban tracks in the suburban Ross Avenue neighborhood east of Dallas, awakening neighbors and drawing an immediate police response. Within an hour, sheriff's deputies arrived with tracking bloodhounds. The dogs followed a scent trail for two miles but lost it on the Katy rail tracks.[68]

The mystery bomber struck again on May 2, this time, mangling a section of track north of Plano. Sheriffs from two counties and police officers from multiple jurisdictions were forced to admit they had, so far, "not obtained anything they can work with."[69] Despite a $500 reward, no trace of the saboteur was ever found, and the traction company never speculated as to a motive for the mayhem. There were no further incidents, and interurban ridership eventually returned to normal.

Dallas would face deadlier dynamite terrorism threats later in the century—union organizing violence, the dry cleaner wars, gangland disputes and responses to racial integration of housing—but the fear of sudden, random, explosive death by dynamite was well-known at the turn of the twentieth century.

———•———

DALLAS HOMEOWNERS WHO REPLACED their old oil lamps with coal gas lamps could boast of brighter illumination, less flickery lighting and eliminating the need for expensive kerosene. City ordinances of the day didn't require licensed plumbers or electricians to perform the work. Installations were often hurried and shoddy, and there were no provisions for city inspections. Tragically, some of those homeowners found that gas lighting brought the danger of suffocation, fires and explosions.

If E.W. Copley's Jungleland Theatre had exploded twelve hours earlier, hundreds of moviegoers and museum visitors might have perished. Instead, the morning gas explosion in January 1912 blew out the front of the theater and upstairs museum; shattered glass and damaged buildings for blocks around; and seriously injured six.[70]

Jungleland Theatre and Museum was modeled after Barnum's New Museum, updated for the twentieth century. On the second floor of the three-story building at 1505 Elm Street, near Akard Street, was the Jungleland Museum and Zoo. The museum featured a menagerie of taxidermied animals from around the world. ("A specimen of every animal that is in existence!" Copley's advertising promised.) Exhibits included living primates, predators, rodents, reptiles and big cats. ("Featuring Sultan, the only lion known to wear glasses and smoke a pipe!") The 700-seat picturehouse on the first floor ran movies continuously, "showing daily not less than three reels of the best pictures that can be obtained." A 112-instrument Welte orchestral organ provided concert-class music between features.[71] A single ten-cent ticket bought admission to both attractions. "A big show for little money," Copley promised.

Copley hired a local handyman to install a gas generator for a private lighting system in the theater. When the workman noticed there was gas leaking into the theater, he opened the front door to let some air in. The

The explosion at Copley's Jungleland attraction sent lions, snakes and monkeys scattering onto downtown streets. There were no human fatalities from the blast. *Courtesy of DeGolyer Library, Southern Methodist University.*

man was standing by the door when the explosion occurred, hurling him against the ceiling and lodging him in the wreckage of the big organ.[72] The explosion and resulting fire injured the workman, a night watchman and four pedestrians who happened to be walking past the theater. All survived their injuries. Many of the monkeys, birds, lions and other exotic animals were killed outright. Some, however, escaped onto Dallas streets and had to be recaptured or shot.[73]

———◆———

THROUGHOUT MOST OF THE first decades of the twentieth century, the gas used for heating and lighting was not the "natural" gas that is commonly used today. (Natural gas was an undesirable byproduct of oil exploration and was often allowed to burn off harmlessly at the well site.) Commercial gas at the turn of the century was most often coal gas, derived from the burning of coal; it was collected and put under pressure. Coal gas and natural gas are invisible and have no detectable smell. Modern producers mix an odorant into the gas and, occasionally, a coloring agent to detect leaks.

A young Dallas schoolteacher had no clue that explosive levels of gas filled her new stove.

Gladys Hurdle was the fifteenth child of parents who had been born into slavery. She attended school in her East Texas hometown and, with financial assistance from her siblings, graduated from Northeast Texas Christian Theological and Industrial College in 1914. After teaching in Timpson for several years, she was elected by the Paris school district to teach there. In 1922, she was recruited to Dallas, hired to teach music and literature to students of the B.F. Darrell School.[74]

Along with seven other schoolteachers, Miss Hurdle found respectable lodging at Cornelia Adams's boardinghouse at 2805 Thomas Avenue, just a short walk to the school at Hall and Lenox Streets and to the Black-owned shops in the neighborhood. In February 1923, Mrs. Adams was converting her boardinghouse to gas heating, and Miss Hurdle's room was the first to have a gas stove installed.

On Monday, February 5, Miss Hurdle rose at first light. The woman in the room below heard her alarm clock ring and the sound of her footsteps walking across the floor to the location of the new stove. The next sound

A gas explosion blew this business to splinters. Compressed gas was an improvement over liquid fuel for heating and lighting, but a lack of inspections led to tragedy. *Courtesy of the Anderson County Historical Commission.*

was a thunderous *whoof*, followed immediately by a floor-buckling explosion and the sound of glass and brick falling. Upstairs residents screamed that the building was ablaze.

Schoolteacher Gladys Hurdle, thirty-two, was the only fatality, though other residents suffered grievous injuries and burns. Fire officials later speculated that improper installation had allowed gas to leak and build up inside the stove and along the floor of her bedroom. The act of striking a match touched off the inferno. The following Friday, a delegation of family members and former Timpson students arrived in Dallas to escort her remains back to East Texas for burial. A choir made up of Darrell School music students sang to Miss Hurdle as her body left Dallas on the train.[75]

———◆———

THE WRECKAGE OF THE Odd Fellows lodge hall was so profound and scattered such a distance that Dallas police and fire commissioner Clarence Parker couldn't attribute a specific cause to the gas explosion of the IOOF meeting hall. The blast killed six and was the deadliest Dallas explosion for the next twenty years.[76]

Members of Metropolis Lodge No. 358 of the Odd Fellows lodge had scheduled their initiation of new members for the night of May 11, 1927. The lodge met on the second floor of a two-room brick building on the northwest corner of Forest and Second Avenues, and a half-dozen members arrived early to prepare for the rituals at 8:30 p.m. The first floor was occupied by three business—a grocery store, a barbershop and a drugstore. The grocery and barbershop were closed for the evening; only the drugstore remained open.

As members and initiates arrived, they waited in an anteroom for the ceremony to begin. One of the members, W. E. Brunson, a Dallas firefighter, thought he smelled smoke and walked downstairs to investigate. Brunson spotted a blue jet of flame coming from a door jamb. He called to the men upstairs, telling them to vacate the building, before rushing to the pharmacy to call the fire department. Other members, fireman W. Henry Lee and Walter H. Coleman, directed streams from hand extinguishers as still others tried to reach the gas meter in the basement of the grocery to shut the gas off.

A chemical fire engine and additional firefighters arrived quickly. Some lodge officers remained in the upstairs office, gathering relics, when Assistant

Fire Chief Jack Redmond ordered them to evacuate immediately. Redmond then ran downstairs to direct his crew and equipment. Jason Euberman was standing one hundred feet west of the building, trying to see what all the excitement was about.

Ka-BOOM!

"The building raised three feet off the ground," Euberman said later. "There was a terrific explosion and a gust of wind that passed my face like a cyclone." The explosion brought Euberman to his knees. The sound of the explosion was heard throughout the county, and debris rained for blocks around. (A motorist several blocks away was pelted by oranges that had been blown into the sky by the blast.) The owner of the Gulf filling station across the street from the building was blown against the rear wall of his office and seriously injured. The two-story building was demolished; nothing was left but a matted heap of bricks and fallen timbers. Within an hour, a crowd of more than one thousand gathered to assist in recovering any survivors from the wreckage. They spent the night under floodlamps that had been installed by the fire department, passing bricks from hand to hand, searching for the dead.

With all the wreckage, Commissioner Parker couldn't determine how the gas had leaked. But he was confident that it "filled every wall and penetrated every crevice" before it ignited and exploded. The six fatalities were: O.D. Allen, a thirty-two-year-old pharmacist who was killed immediately behind his dispensing counter; Frank Linka, twenty-one, who was seen sitting in his parked car, reading a newspaper, when the blast occurred; Mrs. Christina Cour, who was walking home after dinner with friends and happened to be on the sidewalk outside the grocery store; Eddie P. Norvell, who was waiting inside the drugstore, waiting to pick up a prescription for his wife; Fireman W. Henry Lee, thirty, who was a member of the lodge attempting to douse the blaze at the time of the blast; and W.D. "Fatty" Hill, the lodge secretary, who was recovered from the debris hours after the explosion.

———•———

By the 1920s, gasoline was the fuel of choice for most automobiles; internal combustion engines had largely replaced the old steamers and electrics. But refining large quantities of gasoline from petroleum was still a new technology, and the means of delivering and dispensing it were still being worked out.

Early automobiles—particularly, the steam-powered ones—could explode on Dallas streets, killing drivers, passengers and nearby pedestrians. *Courtesy of DeGolyer Library, Southern Methodist University.*

The Simms Oil Company refinery in West Dallas initially shipped gasoline in railcars that were originally intended for water. After each shipment, a worker climbed into the tank car to swab it out. One such worker, H.B. Taylor, was followed by two other workers as he climbed through the car's manhole. Halfway down the metal ladder, he flicked on his electric lantern.

Ka-BOOM!

An apparent short in the lantern ignited the fumes remaining in the tank car, blowing Taylor out of the manhole and onto the ground. His coworkers were seriously injured by the explosion; Taylor didn't survive the night.[77]

Gasoline was delivered to Dallas filling stations in large drums carried on trucks. A.D. Randell of Trinity Heights was leaning on a lamppost at the corner of Commerce and Poydras Streets when a large gravel truck collided with a truck carrying gasoline. The drums exploded, leaving

Randall with burns over his eyes, face and head. (He sued both trucking companies for $10,000.)[78]

A box of dynamite, a stream of gasoline and a fire eating its way to the explosive is the stuff of action movies. In 1927, a filling station attendant opened the spigot on a barrel of gasoline, and his lantern accidentally ignited the fuel. The gasoline ran flaming toward a box of dynamite that was stored in the shop. Firemen arrived in time to douse the dynamite with water and hose down the barrel until the tank's spigot could be safely closed.

Ka-BOOM averted.[79]

———◆———

THE MOST SIGNIFICANT EXPLOSIVE danger to early Dallasites went mostly unnoticed by most residents, hidden in plain sight among the commerce and construction occurring everywhere in the bustling town: steam. It powered trains along the tracks on downtown streets. It drove the heavy excavating equipment used to dig new foundations and powered tall lifts that raised building materials to higher floors. It turned the drill bits used for private water wells. Steam was generated in large cast-iron tubes, boilers where water was contained and heated to create maximum pressure and power.

The night shift operator of one of the White Rock Reservoir's pumps probably overfed the new boiler and dozed off as it overheated. James Murphy was scalded to death when the boiler exploded on him.[80]

The big boilers were nothing short of bombs, waiting to explode at the slightest mismeasurement of water or heat.

In 1910, many of the larger office buildings and hotels drew water from their own artesian wells, assuring a regular supply of water when the city utility was unable to do so. That's why the owners of the Campbell Hotel, located at the corner of Elm and Harwood Streets, hired contractor John Sharpe to drill an artesian well in the narrow alley off Harwood Street that separated the hotel from First Presbyterian Church.[81]

John Sharpe's crew first built a forty-foot-tall timber derrick, placing it about fifty feet into the alley from the Harwood sidewalk. Twenty feet farther, they cradled the boiler on heavy wooden chocks that were anchored to the ground and strapped the twenty-five-foot-long boiler tube to the chocks. The boiler had a square firebox welded to the rear of the tube, where a wood fire would heat water inside the boiler, creating steam to spin a flywheel that would drive a series of leather belts that would, in turn,

These big steam boilers made drilling and construction easier, but they were huge pipe bombs that could level a city block if not constantly monitored and adjusted. *Courtesy of the Clay County Historical Society.*

twist the teeth of the drill bits into the ground beneath the derrick. This particular steam boiler, recently reconditioned in Houston and installed at the site, had a small pressure gauge sticking out from the dome of the cylinder, but there was no relief valve. There was no way to relieve the pressure in case of overheating.

It was Wednesday, July 19, 1911, four days into the Campbell Hotel well job, and Sharp's crew was already dripping with sweat by 11:30 a.m. Four workers on the ground fed cordwood into the boiler's firebox and shuttled pipe along the alley to the derrick as the drill bit crunched downward. A fifth man was high up on the derrick, preparing to add another length of pipe to the stand. Later, the five workers said that their attention was first drawn to the boiler by a sound like a cork popping out of a bottle and the sight of the pressure gauge flying off into the air. Immediately, the boiler began shaking hard enough to snap the straps that were holding it to the chocks.

Ka-BOOM!

With an explosion loud enough to shatter windows, a seam parted at the rear of the tube, and a jet of scalding steam shot out from the gap. The two-thousand-pound boiler launched itself into the air like a rocket. At thirty feet off the ground, the boiler tipped over to fly eastward up the alley. It bulleted through the derrick, splintering the wooden beams into pick-up sticks, and continued toward the alley entrance, losing altitude as it hurtled toward Harwood Street.

Harwood Street, between Elm and Main Streets, carried its usual mix of midmorning traffic. The sound of the explosion froze farmer B.O. Clark's mules, and his wagon jerked to a halt just before he crossed the entrance to the alley. The mules saved his life at the cost of their own. Clark saw only his headless mules fall to their knees. He barely registered the metal missile crossing just feet in front of him, decapitating both animals as it flew by. H.T. Prewitt pulled the emergency brake on his automobile, stopping on a dime. Another three feet and the one-ton metal tube would have slammed into the vehicle. As it was, the boiler flew across the hood, spewing steam and scalding Prewitt's face and hands.

Charlie Carmack and his wife, Mary, delivered butter and eggs from their Mesquite farm to customers in Dallas. At 11:30 a.m., the Carmack's wagon was parked directly across from the alley entrance on Harwood Street. The couple sat side by side on the wagon bench. Behind them, in the wagon bed, crated eggs were nestled in cotton, and the butter was draped in damp dishtowels to keep it fresh. As the boiler flew across Prewitt's automobile, the front end struck Charlie Carmack broadside, carrying him across his wife

Workers, in 1888, buried twenty gallons of nitroglycerine in glass jars three hundred feet below the lush landscape of Dallas's City Park. It's likely still there. *Courtesy of DeGolyer Library, Southern Methodist University.*

and grinding him into the sidewalk and stone of the building beside their wagon. Still jetting steam, the tube flipped, the top knocking a hole four feet deep into the front of Loudermilk's undertaking parlor. Mary Carmack fell into the street, scalded and torn by flying metal. Charlie Carmack died instantly; his wife died later that evening.

Other than some minor burns and a temporary loss of hearing, Tharpe's crew escaped uninjured. The worker on the derrick managed to jump to a hotel window ledge as the tower disintegrated beneath him, and volunteers rescued him shortly after.

———◆———

MORE THAN A CENTURY later, the city may still face an explosive threat from the nineteenth century.

Dallas suffered a water shortage in 1888, and the city decided to drill a well for artesian water in City Park. The well reached a depth of three hundred feet when drillers encountered hard rock. After some consultation, they carefully lowered two ten-gallon glass bottles of nitroglycerine into the shaft to break up the blockage. The nitroglycerine didn't explode. After two weeks of trying (and failing) to detonate the explosive, workers quietly retrieved their pipes and filled the hole. The nitroglycerine could not be recovered.[82] Today, visitors to Dallas Heritage Village are advised to tread softly. Or else, *ka-BOOM!*

4

DEADLY DALLAS ENTERTAINMENT

For more than a century, Fair Park has been a family destination for Fourth of July entertainment. After a day of food, bands and carnival attractions—just as the sun is setting—there are seats in the grandstand for the big fireworks display.

Archie Brown and Tasla Armstrong, both sixteen years old on July 4, 1912, didn't know one another but ended up sitting side-by-side on the second row of the grandstand. Archie Brown was a bit of a celebrity; he had won the Dallas Public School Athletic League chin-up competition at the city's field games the previous year. Tasla Armstrong was the son of German immigrants. As the schoolboys became acquainted, twenty thousand people surrounded them in the stands and on the infield. Fire wheels and fire portraits of the president, the American Flag and a giant Lone Star opened the show shortly after 9:30 p.m. Ground chasers, smoke canisters and mounted flares preceded the big mortar shots, which lofted shells that exploded into colorful bursts high above the spectators.

Shortly before 10:00 p.m., one of the old mortars burst, sending jagged pieces of the iron pipe and the explosive fireworks shell into the crowd. "It is wonderful that none but these two were seriously hurt," Police Chief John Ryan said the next morning.[83] "These two" were Archie Brown and Tasla Armstrong. The mortar shards and explosive shell struck the grandstand between the two boys. Spectators sitting around them had cuts and burns, but both boys suffered grievous injuries to their upper bodies.

Archie was unconscious. A family wrapped him in a blanket and drove him to the Baptist Sanitarium. Tasla was alert and walking about in a daze. "The bones in the little fellow's arm were badly shattered and were sticking through the skin of his arm," a witness said. "The boy begged and pleaded with the owners of several automobiles for help getting to the hospital, but all offered some excuse for not helping the lad. It was the cruelest thing that I ever saw."[84] A German couple heard the boy, placed him in their buggy and drove him to the hospital.

At Baylor, a surgeon was already at work on Archie. His right upper arm was so lacerated that it was necessary to amputate the limb at the shoulder. When Tasla arrived, the surgeon made the same determination. The boy's left forearm was shredded beyond repair; doctors amputated it just above the elbow. The boys were placed in the same hospital room so they could recuperate together.

———•———

LIGHTNING, FLASHING THROUGH A treetop, cut short preparations for a birthday party and snuffed out the lives of David Bettison, eight years old, and Harry Wrather, nine. Three more boys were shocked and burned slightly when a bolt of electric fire struck the homemade soda stand they had ducked under for cover from a sudden rainstorm. Two other boys were inside and escaped injury.[85]

The seven boys, five of whom lived in the 5600 block of Swiss Avenue, had gathered to play before entering the Bettison house for David's birthday party on Saturday, June 2, 1923. Clayton Browne and Hamlet Harrison had built an impromptu soda stand of metal pipes, scrap lumber and some old shingles on the sidewalk under a large elm tree in front of the Harrison home. "We had a case of soda pop and were going to have a good time," said Jack Greenwood. "We were just talking and laughing when something happened."

The Bettison boy was standing under the roof of the stand; Harry Wrather was sitting on the counter. The Brown, Harrison and Greenwood lads were standing under the large elm tree to wait out the rain shower. A rumble of thunder, a bolt of crackling lightning, a shattered treetop, screams from young throats and Bettison and Wrather were killed. Wrather fell forward, off the counter and onto his face. Bettison crumpled in a heap where he stood. "I saw something big and red and long, then heard such a noise,"

Americans, in 1916, were ready to go to war with Germany. Tens of thousands of spectators and marchers crowded Main Street and its sidewalks for the Dallas's Preparedness Parade. *Courtesy of DeGolyer Library, Southern Methodist University.*

Greenwood said. "I saw David fall, and blood come out on his face. "Then Harry Wrather was on the ground, face down, and he was bleeding from his face. I didn't know what happened. I just screamed 'cause I knew something awful had happened."

———•———

AFTER KEEPING THE EUROPEAN war at arm's length with a policy of American neutrality, President Woodrow Wilson acknowledged in 1916 that the nation should prepare for its eventual entry into what would later become known as World War I. Once Wilson belatedly endorsed the overwhelming preparedness sentiment in the country, towns and cities began organizing massive rallies to demonstrate their support. These rallies took the form of "preparedness parades." New York's parade was one of the first and largest. An estimated 150,000 persons representing all walks of life marched through the city in a show that lasted almost twelve hours. Though not as massive, preparedness parades in Baltimore, Philadelphia, Chicago and other cities drew huge, enthusiastic crowds. The Dallas Chamber of Commerce and the city's manufacturers' association set out to make the Dallas parade the largest yet. They set May 30 as the date.

Suddenly, flag makers from around North Texas went into overdrive to supply flags and patriotic bunting. Uniformed military organizations were the first to sign up to march. Veterans groups wanted in. The Hella Temple, Rotary Clubs, Elks and Knights of Pythias pledged drill teams and bands to the parade. Contingents from large Dallas companies, associations and unions signed up to march. Several hundred women staked out their places in the order of march, with chapters from more than two dozen suffrage and temperance groups signing up. High school and college bands tuned up with their instruments and began practicing Sousa marches.[86]

Surrounding cities joined in, too. Garland pledged a delegation of 500 people, half to march and half to view the parade, and 250 union rail workers from Denison bought matching shirts for their appearance in the parade. Denton announced it would send 60 uniformed nurses, and 40 farmers from Ferris planned for the trip to Dallas. Even tiny Ladonia pledged to send 100 people to view the parade.[87]

The weather on May 30 was perfect for a parade: bright and sunny, but not too hot. Marching groups made their way toward Main Street, where parade marshals placed them in order. "At four-thirty o'clock, practically every business house in town closed its doors," a reporter wrote. "Men stopped their daily routine tasks, and the rush of business ceased" as workers streamed out of stores and office buildings to stake out an observation spot of the sidewalk. The *Dallas Morning News* estimated that "an army of more than 20,000 men, women, and boys marched in the parade, and more than 100,000 men, women, and children lined the sidewalks the entire route of the parade and cheered the marchers."[88] Crowds jammed the sidewalks, and others leaned out of windows overlooking the Main Street parade route. A few of the bravest edged out on ledges or found spots on the metal awnings hanging from the fronts of many downtown buildings.

Horace Meyers was watching the parade from the sidewalk across the Schonfelder Building at 1800 Main Street, near what is now the intersection of Main and St. Paul Streets. He noticed a diligent porter shooing spectators off the awning of the building. Every time the porter turned his back, however, more observers would sneak onto that prime viewing platform.[89] Dr. J.T. Watson stood near Meyers. He watched as a person dropped from a window and onto the awning. Seconds later, the metal and concrete awning tore loose from the wall and fell straight down, "like an elevator," on the crowd below.

Without warning, twenty people were crushed under a ton of wood beams, sheet metal, bricks and mortar. J.A. Rawlings, just a few feet away from the crash, turned in time to see two men, two girls and two women crushed by the platform. He and another dozen bystanders rushed to lift the awning off the injured. "The awning was lifted and held up by dozens of willing hands," Rawlings said. I crawled under it and removed five of the injured or dead. Not a sound came from the injured. One little girl tried to say something to me, but I could not understand her."

The little girl was probably Mildred Butler, age eleven, who had come to the parade with her mother, two cousins, and a grandmother who was visiting from out of town. Onlookers carried Mildred into a nearby drugstore, where she died twenty minutes later. Mildred's grandmother, Mrs. F.E. Allen, who was visiting from Birmingham, Alabama, was killed instantly. The other family members lived but fared poorly. Mildred's mother (and daughter of Mrs. Allen), suffered a crushed hip and never walked unaided again. Mildred's cousin Rosine Butler, who was visiting from Rusk, had many of her facial bones crushed.

Mrs. Ray Ferguson broke bones in her right leg and both feet. Mrs. Ferguson's husband was also standing with the group. The falling awning doubled him over backward, breaking his back and crushing his spine. Ray

Ferguson lingered for a while but passed away from his injuries a week later.[90] Albert E. Cannon, a retired grocer, and Al Lott, the Dallas Fire Department chief engineer, died before they could receive aid. Twelve others were injured, though none critically.

The parade was halted at the site of the accident, of course, allowing the first section to continue. Police and firefighters cleared the street of debris in twenty minutes, and the parade resumed. Within a month, the building's owner was served lawsuits, asking for damages totaling more than $250,000.

————◆————

JUST AS TODAY, FAMILY entertainment at the turn of the twentieth century revolved around a special event, a trip or celebration. Families with picnic baskets turned out for the circuses that passed through Dallas, occasional Chautauqua lectures and even a day of political oration at City Park. The attraction of August 27, 1880 was a celebration—if you could call it that— of a particularly ghastly event. And the whole family was invited.

By dawn of that Friday morning, the country people from miles around Dallas were streaming into the city in their buggies, wagons, on horseback and afoot. They were soon joined by the men, women and children of the town. Some of the adults promenaded along downtown streets, some shopped and others chatted with friends and neighbors. Others simply basked in the blue clarity of the cloudless day, despite the rising summer temperature. It was as if everyone was out for a spontaneous holiday.[91]

Near noontime, much of the crowd moved westward out of downtown, toward the Trinity River Bottoms, just below the Texas & Pacific Railroad Bridge. Family groups, neighbors and friends coalesced around a clearing just northwest of (and well in sight of) the Dallas County Courthouse. For those who didn't bring a picnic lunch of their own, there were food vendors selling sandwiches and green corn. A uniformed band played march music, and a man sold colorful paper hats for the children.

At 1:00 p.m., a cheer went up from the crowd standing uphill from the clearing. The cheers were for the appearance of the Lamar Rifles, a spit-and-polish volunteer militia, as they marched escort for the lumber wagon that was leaving the jail and beginning to roll slowly down the bluff. Sheriff's deputies armed with shotguns and city policemen with walnut billy clubs preceded the cart, motioning spectators aside. The wagon and Lamar Rifles traveled through a tunnel of onlookers as they drew close to the clearing.

Sheriff Moon spoke again: "If you desire to say anything to the crowd, you are at liberty to do so." Wright conferred with the ministers for a moment, then turned to the platform railing to say something to the gathered people. His voice was deep and steady, and it carried over the silence of the crowd. "I am Allen Wright, and I am to be hung directly," he said. "I feel that when I take this fall, I will drop right into the arms of Jesus." For five minutes, he extolled God's mercy while warning spectators not to give way to a hot temper. His sermon told of the comfort his faith was giving him, then he seemed to run out of words. "I have no more to say," he ended. "I thank you all for your attention."

Wright shuffled back to stand on the trapdoor, and the clergymen surrounded him. One read Psalm 86 ("For great is thy mercy toward me: and thou hast delivered my soul from the lowest hell"). Another spoke a short prayer. After shaking hands with Wright, the clergymen exited the platform.

With a quiet exchange of words, Sheriff Moon tied Wright's hands behind him and positioned him over the center of the trapdoor. Moon placed the

Even after legal executions were moved inside, away from public view, some officials felt the need to memorialize the events, so the participants and the guest of honor were presented with a photograph. *Courtesy of the University of Texas at Arlington Libraries.*

noose around Wright's neck, adjusting it so the knot was in front of his left ear, and snugged it tight. "Please fix it so it will break my neck," Wright was heard to say. A deputy placed a black bag over the condemned man's head. At 1:45 p.m., Sheriff Moon said, "Goodbye." The word was a signal for the man below the platform to pull a pin. The trapdoor fell open, and Allen Wright dropped into eternity.

Allen Wright's public hanging was a legal execution. Until 1923, Texas law required county sheriffs to execute death warrants signed by a district court judge; the law required that the execution be conducted in the county where the condemned was convicted and in a manner open to the public. Execution was most often done by hanging.

By the turn of the twentieth century, most Texas county sheriffs had concluded that the public spectacle was loathsome and offensive to the community. Under the guidance of the state sheriffs' association, many counties brought their hangings indoors, away from the eyes of the general public and witnessed by invitation only. Association lobbying led to a change in the law, making electrocution the preferred form of execution and designating the state prison in Huntsville the location for the state's only electric chair. Unlike fireworks shows, birthday parties and parades, public hangings as a form of deadly entertainment disappeared from Dallas before the turn of the twentieth century.

DEADLY DALLAS AIRSHIPS

At the beginning of the twentieth century, there was a primal magic to flight that simultaneously awed and fascinated. Popular magazines promised readers that motorized, heavier-than-air flight was possible, and everyone wanted to be the first to prove it.

Humankind always held the sweet dream of soaring like birds. In theory, flight was simple, requiring only a balance of gravity and lift, speed and drag. Find the precise balance, and you're soaring through the clouds. Get it wrong, and you'll find your sweet dreams and flying machines in pieces on the ground—and probably a broken neck, too.

Ignoring the danger and savoring the thrill, every North Texas plowboy with a barn workshop was building his own airship. A particularly eloquent Midlothian farmer promised his device would "take the place of passenger trains and steamships for the conveyance of people." W.D. Custead of Elm Mott announced that his airship was ready to fly, and he invited a newspaper reporter to join him on the maiden voyage. (The weather was never quite right for a flight demonstration.) And an East Texas Baptist minister claimed to have flown fifty yards at the height of about twelve feet in an airship whose construction plans came directly from the Bible.[92]

By the time Orville Wright completed his twelve-second flight at Kitty Hawk in 1903 and demonstrated it in the following years, people were plane crazy. Soon, men in taverns could debate features of the different airships designed by the pioneers: Wright, Curtiss, Langley, Lilienthal and Bleriot. Philanthropists and capitalists offered treasure chests full of prize

Aviator Lincoln Beachey flew this aircraft at the 1914 State Fair, thrilling fairgoers with a series of vertical loops. Two months later, he was dead in a crash. *Courtesy of DeGolyer Library, Southern Methodist University.*

monies to pilots and planes who met performance challenges. Every week, it seemed, airmen set new records for longest distance, flight duration and altitude. Children could recite the names of the famous daredevil aviators—Selfridge, Ferber, LeBlon, Michelin and Roble—as quickly as they recited their ABCs.[93]

Despite the barrels of newspaper ink that were spent on the wonders of aviation, the birdmen and their machines were flying nowhere near Dallas. For most of the first decade of the twentieth century, flyers stuck to their home fields in France, Germany, Great Britain and the Northeast United States. Dallas had yet actually to see the modern marvel of flight.

Railroad millionaire E.H.R. Green drove the city's first production automobile into Dallas in 1899 and was determined to demonstrate one of the new airships for Dallas at the 1909 fair. Green struck out in trying to buy an airship from the Wright Brothers and Glenn Curtiss.[94] Green and the Dallas Chamber of Commerce finally located a pilot willing to perform a flight demonstration in Dallas, and they found him pretty close to the bottom of the barrel. Otto Brodie was a carnival sideshow performer who had just learned to fly, and the Dallas engagement was his first as an aviator.[95] Brodie promised to break the then-current altitude record—4,100 feet—while in Dallas for the four-day demonstration, and he promised provide other sensations. "I will show the people of this section something undreamed of in the way of aerial navigation," he said.[96]

March 3, 1909, was the first day of the air show. An expectant crowd of more than five hundred gathered in the fairgrounds grandstand at 3:00 p.m. to see Brodie, who was still trying to assemble his aircraft. At dusk, Brodie finally rolled down the racecourse, lifted off to about eight feet and ended his flying for the day.[97] The next few days were little better. Brodie made a few hops of up to forty feet and one pass by the grandstands at seventy-five feet. During the third day of this disappointing show, while at an altitude of about twenty feet, Brodie's plane heeled over on its side, turning a tight spiral before crashing into the ground like a busted box kite. People came running from all sides, but Brodie pulled himself from under the wreckage. Aside from a split lip, he seemed uninjured.

The rest of the exhibition was canceled, of course. The pilot's crew packed pieces of the biplane into crates and shipped them back to Chicago for repair. "Daredevil" Brodie departed Dallas on the Saturday night train; the Dallas Chamber of Commerce offered full refunds to anyone who purchased a ticket to the city's first exhibition of heavier-than-air motorized flight. Brodie left town without a paycheck for having failed to meet the performance terms of his contract.[98] Brodie had only shown Dallas its first airplane crash, and even that wasn't very spectacular.

———•———

AFTER THE BRODIE DEBACLE, the Dallas Chamber of Commerce wanted more than ever to stage a real air show—prestigious, sanctioned, competitive, exciting and international. It succeeded ten months later, in January 1911, when it booked the famed Moisant troupe of flyers for a five-day competitive exhibition. John Moisant, an immensely popular airman, was the first to fly across the English Channel, and he had endeared himself to Americans by casually flying circles around the Statue of Liberty in New York harbor. Roland Garros held the French, German and Italian speed records. Archibald Hoxey held the American altitude record of 11,400 feet. Five other experienced airmen were determined to set records of their own in Dallas.[99]

The Dallas air show opened under a black cloud, however, due to the deaths of two of the featured flyers. Moisant, at an air show in Los Angeles, and Hoxey, in New Orleans, were killed in crashes within hours of one another the weekend before they were to appear in Dallas. In the spirit of "the show must go on," two other noted flyers stepped in for Moisant, and the Dallas air show opened as scheduled on January 4, 1911.[100]

The five-day aviation meet—expanded to eight days by popular demand—was an immense success. Despite uncertain weather, the flyers participated in pylon races; competed for altitude, flight time and distance records; and gave the audience chills with a few near-fatal engine failures, crashes and other mishaps. "Twenty thousand people were in the fairgrounds, and probably twenty thousand more stood on sidewalks or on the roofs of buildings" to watch Frenchman Rene Barrier fly over the city. For many, it was the first time they had seen an aircraft, and the sight was thrilling. "The roof of nearly every building was dotted with people, and there were many lodged on the fire escape platforms."[101]

As successful as it was, the air show was responsible for one fatality and three unfortunate injuries. The three-year-old son of Millard F. Horton was leaning out of a second-floor window to catch a glimpse of Barrier's flight above the city when he fell to his death on the concrete below. Three other boys were seriously hurt in separate incidents while trying to fly toy

Miss Matilda Moisant, the Lady Aviator flying over new Live Stock Pavilion in her Monoplane at Fair Park, Dallas.

Matilda Moisant, the sister of the famed flyer John Moisant, headlined a Dallas air show in 1912. Her lavender velvet flight suit, diminutive size, good nature and family name made her a crowd favorite. *Courtesy of DeGolyer Library, Southern Methodist University.*

helicopter-type airships made from plans published on the children's page of the *Dallas Morning News*. Whether due to poor engineering or hasty craftsmanship, the jagged tin rotors flew off their crafts, costing one boy his eye and the others nasty cuts about the face.[102]

———•———

THE JANUARY 1911 AIR show put Dallas in "the throes of a new and decidedly infectious disease—"aeronitis," according to one writer. To see men fly like birds—to soar, to glide, to turn, to loop—sparked in some the same primal impulse that called to Icarus and, in others, the entrepreneurial spirit that drove Croesus.[103] Carpenters, tinkerers and engine mechanics studied the flying machines to see where they could be made lighter, stronger or more powerful. Adventurers and thrill-seekers counted the coins in their pockets and plotted for ways to sit in their own pilots' seats. Capitalists and entrepreneurs analyzed costs and markets to see if there might be a future in manufacturing and selling these airships. Showmen and promoters made lists of the shows and venues where these feats of airmanship could be exhibited to paying audiences. And seventeen Dallas men—moneyed men, with the names of Buckner, Lindsley, Keist, Ling, Sanger, Fretz, Crush and the ever-enthusiastic E.H.R. Green among them—chartered a new organization, the Dallas Aero Club, to seek out business opportunities while promoting aviation in Dallas.[104]

Frederick A. Pine, late of the mining business in Colorado, was one of these entrepreneurs. He plunked down money to buy a Curtiss biplane, leased a field in Oak Cliff, hired a balloon pilot and commenced flight testing in July 1911. Pine's mechanics reverse-engineered the Curtiss machine while he made plans to open his own aircraft manufacturing plant.

Dallas inventor Frank McCarroll arranged to share Pine's leased field to work on a home-built monoplane. A dreamer, McCarroll had studied the flight of birds and aeronautics since before the turn of the century. He had flown gliders in the Trinity River Bottoms as early as 1904, and he patented an invention for retractable airplane wheels based on his observations of how birds "retracted" their feet and legs during flight.[105]

Another young inventor inspired by the 1911 Dallas flying exhibition was nineteen-year-old Harry L. Peyton who, using pictures from aviation magazines and his own math skills, designed, built and flew his own biplane in Dallas in 1912.[106]

The prospect of flight captivated everyone. Young William G. Fuller designed his own aircraft. He later became a military pilot and made a lifelong career in aviation. *Courtesy of the University of Texas at Dallas.*

As early as 1912, Captain J. Hector Worden was scouting by air over battlefields for one or another of the factions engaged in the Mexican Revolution to overthrow President Porfirio Diaz. (His "rank" was bestowed on him by one of the rebel colonels.) Sometime in 1914, tired of being shot at by ground troops, Worden convinced Venustiano Carranza, one of the ascendant rebel generals, to allow him to establish a Mexican air corps. Worden would import aircraft from the United States and train Carranza's pilots. Both men knew the arrangement was illegal; U.S. president Woodrow Wilson had outlawed the sale of war materials to the Mexican rebels. But money was money and flying was flying.[107] Though it was technically smuggling, the sale of guns, ammunition, and even aircraft to the rebel forces was an open secret in Texas. The cross-border benefit to Texas was obvious enough that *Aerial Age Weekly*, a national aviation magazine, remarked that "military activity on the Mexican border is finding a reflection in the development of aviation in Texas."[108]

———◆———

"PERHAPS NO OTHER INVENTION, excepting the automobile, has resulted in as many deaths in so short a time as the airship," the *Dallas Morning News* wrote in an editorial calling for regulation of flying. "Sensitive and sympathetic people are shocked and sickened almost every day by the death of some one or more airmen."[109]

Dallas craved the thrill of flying, and entrepreneurs saw the profits, but the brand-new field of aviation was proving deadly. Even experienced, serious and competitive aviators were dying weekly. (The Aero Club of America compiled a list of forty-one internationally known aviators who had died in crashes in one year alone.) Their airships were experimental, the product of learn-as-you-go engineering; they were fragile, built of varnished muslin and scantling wood. A craft could be brought down by a broken wire, a misplaced strut, a failing engine or even an errant breeze, most often killing the pilot.[110]

Among the 1913 fatalities was that of "Daredevil" Otto Brodie. Never a spectacular flyer, Brodie had earned a reputation for his extreme caution; he was flying at an altitude of just forty-five feet when he was killed. The *Dallas Morning News* noted that Brodie "was the first man to operate an airplane here."[111] Also killed that year was a young military aviator from Virginia, who died during a training exercise in San Diego, one of the fourteen military aviators to die in the previous two years. The aviator was First Lieutenant Moss L. Love, and few in Dallas took notice of his death.[112]

———•———

STUNT FLYER LINCOLN BEACHY drew record crowds to the 1914 state fair, thrilling audiences with his series of loops. His career lasted only four years, however. On March 14, 1915, he died during a performance before a home audience at San Francisco's Pan-Pacific Exposition. As Beachey attempted to pull up and begin his first loop, the wings of his aircraft folded backward like a broken umbrella, and Beachey plunged into San Francisco Bay. His body was later recovered from forty feet of water, still sitting in his cockpit.[113]

Teenaged inventor Harry L. Peyton had the makings of an extraordinary flight engineer and daring aviator. Sadly, he was killed in a crash while leading a group of cadet pilots in 1918.[114]

Dallas city commissioners, in 1915, passed a resolution forbidding Mayor Lindsley from accompanying a flyer on a short demonstration trip into the air. It was too dangerous, they said.[115]

Captain J. Hector Worden, airborne battlefield scout and Mexican gunrunner, returned to Dallas in 1915, intending to become an exhibition airman. Frank McCarroll helped him engineer a monoplane, and Fred Pine built it. On May 6, 1915, Worden was putting the sleek monoplane through its paces, practicing stunts at a field near Vickery Station. Late in the afternoon, Worden climbed to 2,200 feet when he nosed the plane downward, pulling it up into a graceful loop and over onto its back. At the top of the circle, the machine aimed downward again, never swerving as it flew earthward. Spectators saw Worden frantically working the controls as he sped downward. "So terrific was the force of the machine that the large frame was driven fully three feet into the ground," one newspaper reported. "His body was crushed almost to a jelly."[116]

———•———

DALLAS WAS BECOMING RECOGNIZED as the center of civilian aviation in the South. (San Antonio was considered the center of military aviation after the army chose the city as the site of a "finishing school" for aviation students.)[117] After a slow start, aviation in Dallas was certainly developing. A careful count in 1916 would show fourteen airplanes—standard and home-built—in Dallas, at least thirty-five aeronauts, four manufacturing companies and at least six grass airfields. It appeared there was money to be made through aviation in Dallas. "These machines range from the man-carrying 'glider' type to the full-fledged 'battle plane' now in use in the war zone of Europe."[118]

That "full-fledged battle plane" was finding its place in the full-fledged war that was burning in Europe in 1916. Proven in Mexico as an active reconnaissance and communication tool, aeroplanes in Europe were finding roles as bombing platforms and fighters in air-to-ground combat.[119]

In April 1917, after a series of German provocations, the U.S. Congress declared war on Germany, joined its European allies and set about building an army from scratch. By August, the U.S. Army Air Service designated some acreage north of Dallas, near Bachman Lake, as one of it twenty-two aviation training camps. In late October, the army was flying aircraft over the new airfield. They named it Love Field in honor of First Lieutenant Moss L. Love, the seventh military airman to lose his life in a crash.[120] The War Department expected each aviation camp to turn out fifty trained flyers every thirty days. Given the rushed pace and the quality of thrown-together training craft, there were soon airships falling out of the sky all over Dallas.

The U.S. Army built out Love Field as a self-sufficient flight training school, with barracks, hangers, maintenance buildings and classrooms. *Courtesy of the University of Texas at Dallas.*

Love Field pilots were immensely popular in Dallas. These three flyers appear to be taking great pride in showing off their training aircraft. *Courtesy of the University of Texas at Dallas.*

The paint on the support buildings was hardly dry in the first week of January 1918, when Cadet James Dick's flying machine collapsed and fell to the ground just south of Love Field. When the ambulance crew finally reached the site of the accident and pulled Dick from the debris, they found him, at age twenty-two, squashed to the size of a portmanteau. He was the aviation camp's first fatality, and officials chose to name the army's new Dallas Flight Engineering School after him. Camp Dick opened on March 1 at the state fairgrounds with a capacity for two thousand trainees.[121]

For most of 1918, pilot trainees dropped like oak leaves in autumn all over Dallas County. Massachusetts Cadet Victor L. Dennis attempted to make a nosedive landing from an altitude that assured him he would land the hard way. He hit the ground face-first, rupturing the fuel tank. "Almost instantly, Dennis was seared from head to foot with the blazing liquid," said one witness.[122] Cadet R.E. Stall of Detroit was incinerated when his plane crashed near Cochran Chapel, likely due to a broken steering wire. Cadets John Insinger and Earl Zinn were flying in close formation when one turned into the other, causing both planes to crash. Zinn survived his crash, but Insinger didn't. Lieutenant Robinson Bidwell avoided the flames when his aircraft caught fire over Rylie Creek; he leapt from the craft but was killed by the fall. Lieutenant Charles J. Hyde was killed instantly when his plane crashed in a field near Richardson. Lieutenants Parker Bruce and Anthony Sego—trainer and trainee—were conducting a navigation exercise at four thousand feet when their biplane collapsed like a cheap accordion. They fell to their deaths in a field near Letot.[123]

By the time of the November 11 Armistice—a year after Love Field began accepting trainees—eleven flyers had died in aviation accidents. (And that doesn't include ground crewmen who walked into spinning propellers or maintenance workers immolated by spilled and burning fuel.) But the Love Field commander received a decoration for his safety record.[124]

The War Department deactivated Love Field in December 1919, but the army air service continued to maintain it as a supply depot. And military crashes continued.

Edward M. Anderson was shuttling aircraft to from Wichita Falls to Love Field for storage when a wing of his Curtiss JN-4 (Jenny) trainer fell off. The plane dove straight into the ground near Bachman Lake, killing Anderson immediately. Rex Field, thirty, was a Love Field post quartermaster, and he decided to take a Sunday afternoon off for some recreational flying with a friend. The two men flew a leisurely tour of downtown Dallas before returning to the field. At 1,500 feet, the aircraft went into a tailspin, spiraling

Flight students fly in formation above Love Field in their training aircraft. Eleven flyers died during the eighteen months that the U.S. Army Air Service operated Love Field as a training camp. *Courtesy of DeGolyer Library, Southern Methodist University.*

The only wings this trainee earned were angel wings. His body was shipped home to New Jersey after he crashed his aircraft into an Addison cotton field. *Courtesy of the University of Texas at Dallas.*

downward to about 200 feet, where it turned its nose downward and shot toward the earth. Field was killed instantly; his passenger, J.W. Chenoweth of Oak Cliff, survived with a broken arm and some minor bruising. Three army airmen returning a large DH-4 De Havilland observation plane to Fort Sill stopped at Love Field for refueling. An unexpected wind gust at takeoff caught the plane, causing it to turn turtle and crash. The three men were crushed by the fall and charred by flames when the full gas tank ruptured.[125]

The army would maintain a repair depot at Love Field until 1921, but the remaining buildings and property reverted to the Dallas Chamber of Commerce and the manufacturers' association. They arranged for the City of Dallas to lease eighty acres of Love Field as a municipal flying field until the city bought the entire facility in 1927.

The use of aviation in World War I and the commercial possibilities of flight were obvious to business interests in the city. Love Field was touted as the "Flying Center of Texas." The Curtiss Flying School and Curtiss Aeroplane Company opened operations there, as the property attracted aircraft repair companies, flight schools, gas stations, air taxi services and several rudimentary commercial airlines. Love Field also attracted men and women who scraped together a living there doing what they loved best—flying.[126]

———◆———

Thirty-seven-year-old Charles Theodore was a man who lived for flying. Captivated by early flight demonstrations in Dallas, he found himself hanging around flyers, setting chocks, fetching gas cans, helping turn aircraft on the ground or whatever tasks would earn him proximity to the famous airmen. Along the way, Theodore learned to fly and purchased his own airplane. By 1919, he and a partner were making sales, running a repair business, teaching flight and doing a little stunt flying. But Theodore had grander ambitions. He wanted to be the best stunt flyer in the country.

On October 19, 1919, Theodore staged a public demonstration at Love Field. He promised aerial acrobatics, wing-walking, a slide to the tail section and a hand-over-hand return to the landing gear. While Theodore hung from the landing gear, the pilot would execute several rolls and a full loop. Theodore wore a flying helmet and a white scarf as he and the pilot took off in a Jenny-4 two-seater. When the plane reached sufficient altitude, Theodore stood up in the rear seat and began making his way out to the wing. The crowd could see him clearly; his white scarf fluttered out behind him. The daredevil clasped a wing spar and let the air pull his body almost horizontal. Then he released one hand and waved to the crowd.

Theodore returned his feet to the wing and made his way back to the main body of the airplane. On reaching the fuselage, he straddled it and began inching his way back to the tail section. He had affixed a tightrope from the tail wheel to the landing gear axle, and he slipped from the tail section downward, toward the rope, grabbing it before he fell. With the white scarf still fluttering behind him, Theodore began to move hand-over-hand toward the landing gear.

The stunt man had failed to anticipate that his tightrope might stretch under his weight. Halfway to his destination, Theodore found himself at the bottom of a deep "V" in the rope, forcing him to make a vertical climb back to the secure handholds on the landing gear. But he didn't make it. The crowd below screamed as Theodore fell five hundred feet to the ground below, his white scarf fluttering out above him. Oblivious to Theodore's fall, the pilot entered his loop in the sky. "The first information I had on the accident," said pilot H.H. Montague, "was when I looked below and saw the people running to one spot. I knew then that Captain Theodore had fallen."

Theodore's body was discovered in a vacant lot near Wycliff Street and Oak Lawn Avenue. Called to the scene, Dr. A.R. Carpenter "found on examination, practically every bone in the body broken."

The night before his accident, Charles Theodore had visited a reporter at the *Dallas Morning News* offices to invite the public to his demonstration and scare up some publicity. He told the reporter he would "outrival the aerial performances of Lieutenant Locklear."[127] On that fatal Sunday, Theodore had performed stunts from Ormer Locklear's repertoire. The difference was, Ormer Locklear was still alive.

———◆———

ORMER LOCKLEAR WAS A Texas boy, born in Greenville in 1891. He joined the army air service in 1917, later becoming a flight instructor. Locklear was a proponent of wing-walking to make emergency repairs while still in flight. He became proficient at the skill.

After the war, Locklear and two other flyers purchased aircraft and formed the "Locklear Flying Circus." Locklear drew huge crowds performing stunts no one else could do. He did the standard wing-walking, of course, but he

Stunt flying sensation Omer Locklear performs a headstand from his cockpit. The Texan was buried in Fort Worth after he suffered a fatal crash while filming a movie. *Courtesy of the University of Texas at Dallas.*

also perfected a transfer from an automobile to a flying plane, jumping from one aircraft to another in midair and hanging from the landing gear as the plane flew dives, rolls and loops. They earned a national reputation and made the men wealthy. Soon, Hollywood came calling.

Signed to a contract by Carl Laemmle of Universal Studios, Locklear showed off his stunts in *The Great Air Robbery* (1920). The movie earned ecstatic reviews when it opened in Dallas, and the publicity earned Locklear accolades as "the greatest aviation stunt man in the world." Locklear lived the Hollywood lifestyle, dating the famous (and beautiful) Viola Dana (although he already had a wife in Fort Worth). Dana was present for many of the stunts for *The Skywayman* (1920), a William Fox production, and Locklear's first starring role.[128]

Principal photography lacked just one more stunt: a nighttime shot showing Locklear's plane falling and crashing into some oil derricks. Locklear was to pull out of the dive in time to pull up into a loop. Apparently, the spotlights disoriented Locklear, causing him to misjudge his altitude and fly directly into the ground. The crash and a massive explosion killed Locklear and his pilot instantly. Locklear's body was returned to Fort Worth for a funeral service that rivaled Valentino's for attendance and fan hysteria. He was buried in Greenwood Cemetery. (*The Skywayman* premiered in September 1920. Fans loved the movie, especially when the advertising made much to do of the fact that footage of Locklear's death was included in the film.)[129]

——◆——

AERIAL STUNT FLYING WASN'T just a man's game. Several accomplished stuntwomen performed throughout Texas on the fair and rodeo circuit. Cowgirl Florence Hughes proved that riding a bucking bronco is tame when compared to riding a bucking airplane. Her act involved cinching a western saddle to the fuselage of a Curtiss Jenny near the tail and sitting astride it. The plane would taxi around the field at up to thirty miles an hour, then begin a series of abrupt hops. Crowds invariably came to their feet as the plane took off and performed a tight loop with Hughes waving one arm, cowboy hat in hand, and yelling, "Whoopie-ti-yi-yay!"[130]

Aircraft stunt performers would remain a mainstay of state fair programming for much of the 1920s. For several years, stuntwoman Lillian Boyer performed her speeding-automobile-to-airplane ladder transfer four times a day for cheering fairgoers.[131]

——◆——

FOR EVERY TOP-OF-THE-MARQUEE STUNT flyer hogging the big shows, there were a thousand love-to-fly pilots trying to earn a few bucks in small towns at county fairs and local carnivals. Their classified advertisements often filled columns in newspapers with broad statewide coverage. "Aviation brings better crowds," promised one Dallas flyer in the *Dallas Morning News*. "My aviators give satisfaction. Best prices. Night flying, also." The advertisement appeared under the "Privileges for Sale" heading, along with advertisements for trapeze artists, motordrome drivers and freak shows. Below it was an advertisement for Reliable Aviation, using a *News* response box as its address: "Mr. Secretary—If you want an aviator who will fill the bill, get in touch with me. No flight, no pay."

It was with classified advertisements like this that Lester Miller booked his shows.[132] Lester Miller spent much of his life in Dallas, and his aviation career touched about every base (as was typical for itinerant flyers during the first three decades of heavier-than-air aviation). Miller was a mechanic, a builder, an instructor, an entrepreneur and, at times, a smuggler. Above all, Lester Miller was a flyer.

Miller was born in Commerce in 1892, but his family moved from oil boomtown to oil boomtown, ending up near Chickasha, Oklahoma, in 1905. Still in his teens, Miller helped a local bicycle shop owner and tinkerer build one of the first airplanes in Oklahoma: a monoplane called the *Albatross*. By 1911, Miller was flying *Albatross* and other aircraft in exhibitions throughout Oklahoma and Texas. (At some point, he added an *e* to the end of his first name for show business purposes.)[133]

Miller made the rounds of small Texas towns, flying for fairs and town celebrations. He flew a biplane for 150 aging Confederate veterans at a reunion of Hood's Brigade in Calvert. He billed himself as "Professor Lestere Miller" at a Coleman Pioneer Days event. He donned a red suit and beard for Christmas Trade Days in Electra. Meanwhile, he was perfecting his signature crowd-pleasers: the "tango glide," the "dip of death" and "backward spiral."[134] But it was hard to make a living as a flyer. The exhibition season in Texas was just nine months long, if that. And Texas wind conditions—especially during spring and fall—could ground a plane regardless of the pilot's eagerness to fly. After the expense of shipping his plane to Weatherford and paying for accommodation for his mechanic and himself for a weeklong Fourth of July event, Miller was forced to forfeit three-quarters of his fee when the wind and rain kept him grounded. A similar situation in Mesquite earned him a blackball there. "The Commercial Club refused to pay the price, especially in view of the fact that Miller's so-called flights were very unsatisfactory."[135]

Exhibition flyers like Miller loved to fly, but they also learned to supplement their income with other flying-related activities. For a while, Miller worked as chief mechanic and builder for Fred Pine, eventually earning a portion of the company and changing its name to Pine-Miller Aviation. An experimental program by the U.S. Post Office allowed contracts to be issued to independent aviators for intercity mail delivery. On October 4, 1913, Lestere Miller became Texas's first airmail pilot when he snagged the contract for delivery between Brownwood and Comanche.[136]

Ten thousand thrilled spectators came out to see their first airmail delivery. Miller was flying at three thousand feet over the crowd when a fuel line broke, and his engine wound down to a full stop. The aircraft's nose tilted downward toward the multitude as a composed Miller went into his "dip of death." Just before striking the earth, he leveled off, using his "tango glide" to bleed off speed for a safe and gentle landing in a nearby hayfield. It was one of his best exhibitions of trick flying yet, and he wasn't even paid for it.

Miller spent the rest of his life promoting himself as a flyer. In 1959, at sixty-three years old, he was invited to display his original 1911 Curtis biplane at the opening of Big Town Mall in Mesquite. He entertained crowds with stories of early aviation exploits, most of them true. Miller died of natural causes in 1963, with most of his bones still attached one to the other.[137]

———•———

IN THE EARLY DAYS of flight, so the stories go, someone asked Wilbur Wright whether the dangers of aviation could ever be eliminated. He answered that, over time, all risks could be removed, except for one—the grandstand. Aviation had become progressively safer during the first two decades of manned flight. Aeronautics had become a science; materials consisting of the perfect balance of durability and weight had been identified; and pilots were more experienced. By the 1920s, people were beginning to trust their mail and themselves to flying machines. But every flying stunt man, every daredevil pilot, every ill-trained student and every pilot of an untested machine who plowed into the ground from one thousand feet eroded that trust.

The entrepreneurs who had spent fortunes building businesses around aviation needed the general public to trust in the safety of flight. The businesspeople needed the risk-takers to disappear. The trouble was, there were no regulations to govern civilian flyers. A pilot could take to the air in a ramshackle aircraft and fly the length of Commerce Street at ten feet above traffic without breaking the law. "Until Congress agrees on some standard laws to govern these cases, then the cities and states of this country ought to take some action to protect the public." The *Dallas Morning News*, ever mindful of the city's aviation business interests, editorialized for greater regulation of civilian flight. In 1924, Dallas city commissioners were considering action on a slate of flight regulations.[138]

The regulations came too late for two Southern Methodist University (SMU) students.

Years later, Ainsley E. Stuart would be a lieutenant colonel in the air force, a senior pilot with more than 6,600 hours in the air. In 1924, he was a student at the Love Field Aviation School, the owner of a well-worn war surplus Curtiss Jenny, scrambling to sell flights to pay his tuition.[139] On Monday, April 14, 1924, Stuart had paid (or bartered with) the owner of an open lot

The Semi-Weekly Campus

Volume IX   SOUTHERN METHODIST UNIVERSITY, DALLAS, TEXAS, WEDNESDAY, APRIL 16, 1924.   Number 43

STUDENT KILLED–ONE HURT IN CRASH

Students Investigate Party and Two Dinkeys

Two SMU students, one from Dallas and the other from Oklahoma, paid two dollars each for an aerial tour of the campus. Only one lived to tell about it. *Courtesy of DeGolyer Library, Southern Methodist University.*

behind the SMU Kappa Alpha fraternity house to use the area as a landing strip. He was charging students two dollars each for a flight over the campus, out to White Rock Lake and back to the makeshift landing field. Business that spring afternoon was brisk.[140]

Around 5:00 p.m., two students approached Stuart and asked for a ride. One was a woman named Annie Shaw, the twenty-four-year-old daughter of a dry goods merchant from Ada, Oklahoma, a sophomore and a member of the Pi Beta Phi sorority. The other student was Hunter Temple, a freshman, recent graduate of the Terrill School and an aeronautics enthusiast. Temple came from a well-known family, the only son of S.A. Temple, the president of Dallas Trust & Savings Bank. The old aircraft had two cockpits, one for the pilot and one for the trainee, both with flight controls. Stuart wedged both students into the forward cockpit for a better view while he flew from the rear.

On takeoff, Stuart rose slowly—just enough to clear the few buildings— and flew south, toward Mockingbird Lane. At the south end of the campus, he turned to the north, flying parallel to Hillcrest Road on the left and the SMU women's building on the right at an altitude of about one hundred feet. They flew next to Dallas Hall, the right wingtip level with the very top of the rotunda. As the campus disappeared behind them, Stuart made a sharp bank eastward, toward White Rock Lake. Perhaps the turn was too sharp, or perhaps, as experienced pilots speculated later, the plane was out of balance due to the weight of two passengers in the front cockpit. Whatever the reason, the plane nosed over and crashed to the ground near the intersection of Lovers Lane and Airline Road.

Nearby residents, SMU students, and the SMU night watchman ran to the crash site to render aid. Ainsley Stuart was conscious and attempting to free himself from the wreckage when the crowd arrived. The other passengers appeared lifeless. Two men pulled Annie Shaw from the plane and loaded her into a passing laundry truck that sped her to Baylor Hospital. The front end of the aircraft had folded back over the front cockpit, pinning Hunter Temple under the engine, entangled in wires. His clothing was soaked in gasoline, and onlookers feared he would burn to death if a spark ignited the fuel. A Highland Park fire crew arrived and hosed down the wreckage. They lifted the motor off of Temple's body and clipped the wires that were trapping him. It was evident at the scene that he was dead. Annie Shaw suffered a fractured skull and remained in a coma for two days. The pilot's right leg was broken, and he was released from the hospital that evening.

The following day, SMU vice president H.M. Whaling announced that he would not ban airplanes from flying from or over the campus. Automobile accidents, while frequent, were not a deterrent to driving, Whaling said. Students would need to exercise their own judgment as to future airplane flights.

———◆———

AS THE NEW CENTURY progressed, Dallas's Love Field became a great regional municipal airport. General aviation migrated from Love Field to new dirt-runway flying fields on the outskirts of the city. Flying became safer with the congressional passage of the Air Commerce Act in 1931 and the Civil Aeronautics Act in 1938.[141]

6

DEADLY DALLAS DISEASE

Dallas spent two decades nailing down the perfect job description for the city scavenger. The city kept growing, and so did the need for proper scavenging.

From 1882 through the early 1900s, the Dallas City Board employed a city scavenger, a person whose job it was to assure sanitary conditions in the city and to remove garbage. It was a position that grew and changed as the city grew along with the recognition that refuse and filth fostered disease.[142]

The primary job of the first city scavenger was to remove dead animals from the city's streets and alleys. Before the automobile took over the streets completely, Dallas was a four-legged town. Horses, mules, oxen, cattle and other large livestock lived within the city. When a horse died, some were tempted to drag the cumbersome carcass to a nearby vacant lot for whatever scavengers wanted it. Besides creating an odor nuisance, the decaying body of such a large animal could feed and foster millions of disease-carrying insects and pests. Instead, the city scavenger would cart the dead animal to a rendering plant, city landfill or, later, the city crematory. The ordinance also required the city scavenger to clean the public privies and remove any slop or filth as requested by a resident.

At first, city scavengers were paid a pittance as a salary, but they also earned a payment for every pound of dead horse or privy filth they delivered at the end of the day. The city employees learned they could pad their income by hiding lead weights or even anvils under the noxious messes. A later city scavenger was discovered selling the meat of freshly deceased animals to unscrupulous butchers to earn a few extra bucks. (As freelancers tried to horn in on his animal removal business, City Scavenger B.H. Hayward placed advertisements saying he was the only one authorized by the city to remove dead animals and that any interlopers could "see me at the calaboose, as the law directs.")[143]

Even after the city passed an ordinance in 1887 requiring that all garbage left on the street "be placed in a barrel or galvanized can with a close-fitting top," trash still piled up on city streets. "The *News* has received many complaints from citizens, who tell of piles of garbage and vegetable refuse," the *Dallas Morning News* noted. "This proves that citizens, at least, are wide awake to health and cleanliness."[144]

An ordinance in 1894 established an official office of city scavenger. It was likely a patronage job with a salary and a city office. The first head of the office was Tom Larkin, a former transit motorman who could charge city residents ten cents for every square foot of "night soil, privy filth, etc." hauled away. Larkin was authorized to hire a corps of scavengers and pay them all or part of what Larkin collected for himself. (It was a job rife with possibilities for personal enrichment. A later city scavenger was said to be taking home $25,000 a year.)[145]

Dallas eventually abolished the office of city scavenger in 1908, contracting trash collection services to an outside firm. Lobbying for improved sanitation and better health, groups such as the Cleaner Dallas League, Dallas Federation of Women's Clubs and Civic Improvement League convinced the city to return trash collection to direct council control.[146]

———•———

DESPITE THE BEST EFFORTS of its city scavengers, Dallas was teeming with disease-carrying filth at the turn of the twentieth century. In 1900, fewer than half of the city's residences had toilets—indoors or out—that emptied into the rudimentary Dallas sewer system. Most residents used communal "dry closets," where waste was deposited into a bucket and each user had to cover their donation with a scoop of sand or lye from a nearby pail. Others used unlined pits, allowing the waste to compost in place and seep into the groundwater.

Dallas survived from drought to drought, but for several years prior to the turn of the century, it appeared that water from artesian wells might provide all the water the city would ever need. But when the wells tapped out, the city built a series of impoundment lakes—Exall, Bachman's and White Rock—to meet the city's needs with water saved from the wet months. The lakes captured runoff from rains—runoff that included particles of animal waste, human waste and all manner of curbside garbage. All water sources in turn-of-the-twentieth-century Dallas were suspect, but the river next to the city itself was the worst.

On a morning in February 1887, a *Dallas Morning News* reporter noted "a great abundance of fish being hawked through the streets" and decided to investigate the source. It didn't take long to discover that the fish being sold for Dallas dining tables were "floaters," dead fish from the Trinity River that had been killed by the runoff from recently burned warehouse buildings on Commerce Street. "The poisonous properties that slew the fish were whiskey and tobacco," the reporter observed.[147]

When the city's health officer referred to reports of a filthy Trinity River as nothing but "newspaper flourish" in 1891, the *Dallas Times Herald* sent a reporter to walk the riverbanks. "For ten miles down from Dallas, the river is in horrible condition," the reporter wrote. "Its banks are strewn with filth, the surface of the water is covered with floating filth,

Boating and fishing on the Trinity River was an unpleasant experience. The river moved at a sluggish 1.5 miles per hour, raw sewage floated on the river's surface and the smell was unbearable. *Courtesy of the Dallas Public Library.*

the river is full of filth for miles. It is nothing less than a contaminating slough of filth."[148]

Dallas's Trinity River remained a cesspool for the next thirty years. A convenient depository for waste of every kind. In 1925, the state board of health stepped in, conducting a yearlong survey of how Dallas had befouled one of Texas's major rivers. The final report was brutal, declaring the river water "deadly," and it concluded that the waterway was far beyond repairing itself.[149] "The sluggish waters of the Trinity River do not move with sufficient velocity to carry off all the sewage and waste dumped into the channel," the study said. Vegetables irrigated with Trinity River water were found to contain all manner of potentially deadly viruses and bacteria. Cattle from fields abutting the river were wading into the water, causing infections that could spread dangerous pathogens if they were butchered for food. The river water could contaminate the udders of dairy cattle, resulting in the spread of typhus to children. The dirty, sluggish water was a mosquito metropolis, a massive breeding ground for malaria and dengue fever.

"The Sewer Called Trinity River" headlined the first of a series of pointed editorials in the *Dallas Morning News*. Only after the Texas Board of Health report, constant editorializing and pressure from Austin did a consortium of business leaders and politicians muster the political will to clean up the river. Three years later, the city broke ground on a levee project intended to heal Dallas's diseased river.

———◆———

AT THE TURN OF the twentieth century, Dallas had a significant four-legged population. Consider the horse. The county in 1900 had up to fifty thousand horses, many of them stabled in the city. Every horse generated five to ten pounds of manure and a gallon of urine each day. Do the math. Much of that waste was deposited on city streets, mixed into dirt roads and, as dust, blown into homes and restaurants. Butcher shops and produce stands, where uncovered food was displayed, got a daily dusting, too. And that doesn't account for the waste produced by other livestock or for the pigs, goats and chickens kept by many city residents. Animal waste can carry bacteria and parasite eggs that survive in dry conditions, only to reanimate when provided a damp environment. Barefoot children were particularly susceptible to roundworm and toxoplasmosis.[150]

As many as one dozen fire horses might have been stabled together at a Dallas firehouse. A case of rabies in one horse would have imperiled them all, rendering the fire wagons useless. *Courtesy of DeGolyer Library, Southern Methodist University.*

But rabies was the animal disease most people feared. Raccoons, skunks and possums were common sights in the city, and deer, foxes, coyotes and wolves lurked on the outskirts. All of them could infect the beloved household dog or the trusted carriage horse with just a nip or a lick of saliva.

On July 19, 1902, Mayor Cabell called a special meeting of the city commission to deal with death of George, a fire horse of Fire Station No. 2 who had apparently died of rabies. George's passing caused considerable stir in the ranks of the fire department for two reasons. First, it was uncertain whether George might have infected other horses at the station. Second, George's saliva had sprayed several firemen on their scratches or open wounds. The consequences were serious. A whole stable of trained fire horses would have to be destroyed if George had spread the infection, a considerable expense. The firemen also feared for their own lives. Dallas had no rabies antiviral serum available.[151]

The rabies virus attacks the human nervous system. After initial symptoms similar to a common cold, it attacks the brain and can lead to "mad dog" behavior: excitation, drooling, confusion, jerky movements and aggression. In a matter of days, the crazed victim dies with their jaws snapping like an alligator, trying to take a bite out of anyone nearby.

Chickens, eggs, butter and milk came from growers in surrounding areas, who would bring their products into the city for sale to individuals or establishments. *Courtesy of Historic Mesquite Inc.*

After consultation with the commission, the mayor dispatched the city health officer by express train to St. Louis with George's iced head for proper diagnosis. The health officer was to return immediately with the Pasteur antiviral serum to treat the possibly infected firefighters.

The city passed its first pet licensing ordinance in 1871, but it was mostly ignored. From time to time, the city held unlicensed dog roundups; one city dog catcher asserted as fact that "large numbers of dogs of ripe experience left the city every year as soon as the dog wagon made its appearance and remained away until the dog catching season was over."[152] Through most of the 1920s the city averaged ten to twenty cases of rabies monthly. In 1926, the county health officer reported the number of active cases but said it "is was not of such proportion as to threaten to become an epidemic."[153]

---◆---

THE CITY WAS ENCIRCLED by farms that found a voracious market in Dallas for meat, eggs, milk, fruits and vegetables. Cattle, hogs, sheep and rabbits were brought to the city and sold to butcher shops, which processed the livestock and sold the meat, piece by piece, to residents and restaurants. Homes that didn't raise their own chickens readily purchased eggs and poultry from farmers who sold them from open wagons on the streets. In 1900, Dallas registered 146 dairies, most of which processed their own raw milk and sold it in the city. Much of the city's food supply depended on healthy animals, cleanliness and consistent refrigeration of the products as they traveled from farm to table. However, unsanitary water, diseased animals, careless food preparation and poor refrigeration resulted in

Pitchford's market was a respected business, but uncertain refrigeration, open windows, insects and road dust could taint the meats the family butchered and sold. *Courtesy of the Dallas Public Library.*

recurring epidemics of typhoid and cholera in Dallas at the turn of the twentieth century. Despite increasing medical knowledge of the diseases and strong recommendations from the Texas State Health officer, Dallas did not pass significant ordinances requiring the inspection of food establishments and food handlers until 1909.[154]

———◆———

IT'S HARDLY NECESSARY IN the present day to describe the effects of an epidemic of an incurable disease: the fear, isolation, quarantine and, finally, the deaths of loved ones shivering in their beds like pups, their fire burning lower and lower. In the decades on either side of the turn of the twentieth century, Dallas suffered serious epidemics of deadly diseases that, today, are hardly footnotes in medical texts.[155]

Smallpox swept through Dallas in 1882, 1889 and 1898 and caused more than seven hundred cases in 1907, when officials began enforcing the compulsory vaccination of public-school children. The disease returned in 1919 and 1928, each time, requiring strict quarantine procedures. "When we came to Dallas in 1898," an early resident recalled, "the smallpox was really bad. There was a pesthouse you could go to, or else you could stay home and have a yellow flag on your house. We were surrounded by yellow flags."[156]

Dallas constructed a pesthouse for use during infectious epidemics. It was a place for infected people who had no one to care for them; they were to stay there while the disease ran its course. While the place was more of a bunkhouse than a hospital, doctors and nurses visited regularly and provided care. If you chose to quarantine at home, you could fly a yellow flag from your front door, an international maritime symbol for plague and quarantine. (In later years, the city replaced the flags with a large "QUARANTINE!" signed nailed to the front of the house. Caught breaking quarantine? Police were authorized to march you off to the pesthouse for the duration of your illness.)

A particularly virulent form of measles struck in Dallas in 1924, resulting in closed schools and many closed businesses. In the first three weeks of February alone, the city charted 3,900 cases and 18 deaths. The eventual toll would be triple that.[157]

Left untreated, diphtheria can result in breathing problems, heart damage, nerve damage and death. There was no medically proven cure for diphtheria during the Dallas outbreak in 1892, but that didn't stop druggists from hawking such patent medicines as Brown's Bronchial Troches or Darby's Fluid. ("To prevent diphtheria, smallpox, scarlet, typhoid, or yellow fevers, use Darby's.") A vintner placed advertisements in Dallas papers, promising that "diphtheria is cured by the use of Cook's Extra Dry Champagne as a gargle. Ask your physician to try it!" Physicians eventually developed a curative serum, but another diphtheria epidemic swept Dallas in 1930.

Tetanus rarely reached epidemic proportions, but it was a constant presence in the pre-antibiotic days. Death by lockjaw was most prevalent in the city's poorer and rural areas, where children often ran without shoes in the summertime and farmers were more likely to be cut or scratched by rusty implements.

Meningitis is particularly horrifying because it so often affects youngsters. Even those who survive the infection—35 percent of those who contracted the disease during the epidemic of 1911–12 did not—were left with lifelong deformities or debilities.[158] Viral meningitis causes an inflammation of the membranes surrounding the brain and spinal column, and it begins simply enough. The youngster wakes up complaining of a stiff neck and headache. Although showing a slight fever, the youngster seems well enough

Parkland Hospital was a gleaming addition to the city's medical community in 1894, but the seriously injured and ill had to survive a rough buggy ride to reach the hospital. *Courtesy of Historic Mesquite Inc.*

to go to school that day. By afternoon, the headache is worse and may be accompanied by nausea and vomiting. At dinnertime, the child is confused and has difficulty concentrating. Exceedingly drowsy, the youngster goes to bed early, only to waken the household that night with seizures. Chances are that four out of ten such children would be dead by breakfast. There was no sure cure.

On December 31, 1911, a Dallas newspaper listed nine individuals who had died the previous day in its "Local Deaths" column. Of the nine, four had succumbed to meningitis, and all four were under twenty years of age.[159] The disease raged through the city for the next month, and fatalities mounted. Schools delayed their return from the holiday break, church services were canceled, city offices closed and court appearances were postponed. The city health officer reported 185 cases and a 50 percent death rate, but several local doctors said they thought the number of cases was twice what was reported.[160]

Around the nation, Dallas was reported to be a plague city. "Siege of Meningitis Holds Dallas in Terror," one newspaper reported. "A New York man who arrived in Dallas today was very much surprised to find business going on in the normal way," according to a newspaper account. "He said that on the way from New York, he heard and read so much about the terrible epidemic that, if his business hadn't been urgent, he would have turned back at St. Louis."[161] Eventually, though, the epidemic subsided and time passed, leaving only the historical record of a much deadlier Dallas at the turn of the twentieth century.

DEADLY DALLAS FIRE

Thirty-one-year-old spinster Effie Gaines lived with her mother on the upper floor of a two-story East Dallas home that had been divided for use by two families. Effie's mother owned the residence at 740 Roseland Avenue; Mrs. R.T. Parrish and her aged father, Mr. Meyers, occupied the lower floor.[162] The Gaineses' workday morning routine never varied: the women would rise at 5:15 a.m., and Mrs. Gaines—still in her gown and housecoat—would prepare breakfast while Effie dressed for her job at the telephone office. The women lived comfortably on Effie's salary and the rental income. They had recently bought a new icebox and were considering the purchase of a new stove. (Their old kerosene stove required daily priming and the application of several matches before it would light.)

On Thursday morning, April 14, 1909, Mrs. Gaines set eggs and a side meat on the counter, then turned to light the stove. From her bedroom, the younger woman heard an explosive *fwooomp* and saw a reflected flash of light. Rushing toward the kitchen and her mother, Effie felt the heat grow more intense with every step. She turned the corner to see the kitchen bathed in flame, her mother's cotton housecoat and gown burning like a torch. The women attempted to run to the stairway, but exploding kerosene from the stove had set the walls and floor on fire, cutting off their escape. One of the women raised a window, and Mrs. Gaines, still enveloped in flame, jumped through it.[163]

A neighbor who watched Mrs. Gaines tumble from the second-story window compared it to a ball of flame falling to earth. The ball of flame

A boy stands by as firefighters try to save his house. Open flames were ever-present dangers in Dallas homes, often causing fires that took property and lives. *Courtesy of the Fire Museum of Texas.*

landed at the feet of Mr. Myers, the old gentleman from downstairs, and he ran into the house for a blanket to smother the flames as Mrs. Gaines screamed and writhed on the ground. A moment later, Effie, her hair and gown ablaze, threw herself from the same window. Mr. Meyers rolled both women in his blanket, eventually extinguishing their flames.

Neighbors carried the mother and daughter to a house across the street and summoned physicians. Examining them, doctors could find no spot on Mrs. Gaines's body that wasn't horribly blistered or burned black; Effie's hands, face and back were charred, and she had fractured her ankle in the fall. Injections of morphine eased Effie's pain somewhat, but Mrs. Gaines screamed in agony before passing away eight hours later. Her daughter slipped into delirium, though she eventually recovered with gruesome facial scars and without the use of her right hand.

Fire was a horrendous—but not unfamiliar—way to die in Dallas.

———•———

A MODERN-DAY VISITOR TO turn-of-the-twentieth-century Dallas would be astonished by the presence of open flames everywhere. Most large commercial buildings housed giant oil- or coal-fired boilers to provide heat; smaller businesses kept the ubiquitous potbellied stove burning during winter months. Many businesses had converted to pressurized gas jets for interior lighting, but others still relied on coal-oil (or kerosene) lamps. Even the new exterior electric arc lights provided illumination by flashing a powerful open spark between two electrodes. Many specialized businesses required flames to operate: the smithy to soften metal, the candy manufacturer to bring the ingredients in his giant copper kettles to a boil, the restaurant operator to grill his steaks and chops and the newspaper to melt its lead type each day so it could be recast for the next edition.

Open flame was always present in city residences and rural farmhouses as well. Oil lamps provided nighttime and early-morning lighting; some families left unattended lamps burning all night. Most women cooked on wood-burning or kerosene stoves; wash water and bathwater were often heated in large tubs fired by burning wood. Families disposed of their trash in backyard pits, sprinkling it with gasoline and setting it on fire. Even wagons and carriages were equipped with fireboxes to keep passengers' feet warm on winter drives.

When these flames escaped, the results were often tragic, made more so by the materials of the time. Frilly fashion provided a dozen fuses to spread fire over an entire garment, especially when that garment was made of

Early firefighting equipment was primitive, often consisting of firehoses, ladders, axes and enthusiastic firemen, and they were all rushed to the scene of a fire in a horse-drawn wagon. *Courtesy of the Fire Museum of Texas.*

loosely woven cotton or other natural material. Heavily oiled pinewood floors, furniture and cabinetry could ignite with just a spark; untreated wood siding, framing and roofs—particularly after drying for several years in the arid Texas heat—would burn like kindling. Fire could strike with the speed of a viper, and the careless paid an excruciating price.

———•———

Doing the wash was a twice-a-week chore for the mother of a new baby girl. Seventeen-year-old Mrs. Vesta Boatner of 4018 Main Street would haul her wash kettle to the backyard and hang it on a grate. After filling the pot with water from buckets, she would lay firewood beneath it and light the fire. A few splashes of kerosene would bring the fire to full flame. From her sitting room on the afternoon of July 30, 1914, the Boatners' next-door neighbor saw the young mother go into her backyard to prepare the wash. Soon after, the neighbor heard a sound like a pistol shot—the sound of the kerosene can exploding. "Then I saw Mrs. Boatner running for my house, screaming for help." Vesta Boatner was aflame from hair to ankles. "I ran to her with a bucket of water, with which I succeeded in checking the flames. Then, I threw a quilt over her. She was horribly burned."[164]

Vesta Boatner's flesh was burned almost to a crisp from her legs upward. The city hospital physician who examined her said her death was just a matter of time. He did what he could to ease her suffering, but no other treatment was possible. Her husband and daughter accompanied Mrs. Boatner's body home to Mississippi, where she was buried with her family.[165]

———•———

Especially tragic was when the fire fiend claimed children, not because of their carelessness, particularly, but due to their ignorance of the acute danger those open flames represented.

Five days before Christmas in 1899, three-year-old Bertha Ray Freshman was playing inside her house on Patterson Avenue, mimicking the housekeeper who was dusting and sweeping. When the housekeeper stepped out of the room, Bertha picked up a little broom and began sweeping. The housekeeper returned just a moment later to see "the broom and the little girl's clothing ablaze, probably set on fire by the stove. The housekeeper doused the girl with a bucket of water and wrapped her in a blanket, but she was already terribly burned.[166] The housekeeper summoned a physician, and the physician summoned Bertha's father. When he arrived, a writer said, "she tried to stretch out her little baked arms to him, but the effort was too much." Bertha died less than an hour after her accident, saying only, "I am going to see my mama."

In 1914, at the Scott house on Cedar Springs Road, just outside the city limits, twelve-year-old Clara Scott was helping her five-year-old sister, Maggie, make candy on the kitchen stove. Their mother was in the front room, speaking to a neighbor. She heard the explosion from the kitchen and ran there to see her daughters covered with molten sugar and enveloped in flame. The mother suffered frightful burns trying to extinguish the flames.[167] Two days later, on Friday, August 7, 1914, Mr. E.W. Scott and his bandaged wife buried their two daughters at Grove Hill Cemetery.[168]

———◆———

THE LOSS OF LIFE brought about by open flame can hardly be appreciated by twenty-first century Dallasites. Equally hard to comprehend is the primitive state of firefighting manpower, apparatuses and infrastructure at the beginning of the twentieth century. The fires of 1902 demonstrated just how destructive those shortcomings could be.

The fall and winter of 1902 had been exceptionally dry, with no snow and little rain. Spring looked to be the same. Untended grasses were parched, and even new growth curled brown at the edges. Desiccated foliage, gusty March winds and crowded frame houses combined on the night of March 6 and resulted in the area's first major fire of the year.[169]

Shortly before midnight, volunteer firefighters in Oak Cliff—the community had not yet been annexed by the City of Dallas—called the South Dallas Fire Company, asking for help with several out-of-control residential fires. The Dallas firemen harnessed their horses to a new hand pump and galloped off through the night toward Eleventh Street in southeast Oak Cliff. By the time the Dallas fire team arrived, six houses were in flames, wooden fences surrounding the cottages were burning and grass fires edged toward two more residences, blown by a stiff breeze. The area was lit by two flaming telephone poles that burned like twenty-foot-tall torches. Volunteers were manning a water bucket line, fighting a losing battle to prevent the spread of flames.

A new steam pumper allowed firefighters to draw more water at a faster rate. It was of little use, however, when the mains couldn't deliver enough water. *Courtesy of the Fire Museum of Texas.*

The Dallas firefighters quickly dismounted their hose cart, unreeled their two-and-a-half-inch hoses and connected them to water main attachments. It was then that they encountered a problem that doomed area buildings for much of the next decade: lack of water pressure and water.

The Oak Cliff water system depended on a gravity feed and the uncertain pressure of artesian wells; no pumping stations forced water through the pipes. Many houses maintained pumps and small cisterns to provide some pressure for the residence, but generally, system pressure depended on impounded city water. That night, there was insufficient pressure in the main to force water through the firehoses. The Dallas steam pumper was intended to solve low pressure problems, literally sucking water from the city water mains, but it could only work if the mains provided enough water. Oak Cliff—and much of early Dallas and its adjacent communities—built out its early water system using two-inch clay pipe. Even with the steam pumper sucking water from the main, there wasn't enough water available to fully inflate the firehoses. "The water pressure was very light," said Dallas fire chief Magee. "It wouldn't throw a stream to the roof of a one-story house."

By dawn, the winds had died down and firefighters could eventually extinguish the blazes. In all, ten houses and all the outbuildings—almost two city blocks—were nothing but ashes and char. The burned telephone poles and lines disrupted phone service between Oak Cliff and Dallas for a week.

The first Dallas firefighter to lose his life in the line of duty was John Clark, who died in 1902 while trying to apply a chemical retardant to slow the progress of a residential fire. *Courtesy of the Fire Museum of Texas.*

"We found it impossible to do anything to check the fire," Chief Magee said. "It just burned itself out."

Arid conditions kept the Dallas Fire Department busy throughout the March 1902. On the evening of March 18 alone, firefighters scrambled to respond to four fires. They fought two residential fires—one on South Ervay Street and the other on Live Oak Street—extinguishing them before they spread to adjoining residences. A fire on Commerce Street that afternoon sent a woman running from her residence, dragging two children and screaming for help. She saved the children but sank to the ground at the feet of the firemen, dead of an apparent heart attack. At the Dallas Book Company on Main Street at 7:00 p.m., a faulty electric light set fire to loose paper; the flames consumed most of the company's stock but didn't spread beyond the business.[170]

A month later, with still no appreciable rain or relief from the heat, Dallas experienced what firefighters later referred to as the "infernal night." A 3:10 a.m., an alarm called Main Street Firehouse men and equipment to Dorsey

Printing Company on Elm Street (Between Griffin and Lamar Streets). The fire started in a defective electrical junction box and spread quickly through the entire three-story building. Flaming bits of posters, handbills and other printed materials floated into the air, threatening to ignite other buildings. Soon after his arrival, Chief Magee issued a general alarm, summoning every available fireman and piece of equipment from throughout the city. The arrival of an aerial truck from the central fire station allowed firemen to extend their hoses and wooden ladders to the building's upper floors. Within minutes, however, the ladders began to smoke and burn. The ladders collapsed, throwing four firemen into telegraph wires, where they made a circus-like descent, unharmed.[171]

Dozens of brass nozzles directed thousands of gallons of water onto the fire, but it appeared to be spreading to a wallpaper plant next door. Fire Captain Tom Meyers was directing one of the streams of water when a section of the Dorsey building collapsed, showering him with brick. Magee reached him first, pulling the bloody man clear of the wreckage and calling for transport to a hospital.

After almost an hour of desperately trying to contain the flames, Chief Magee spotted a dull red glare to the northwest, the sign of another fire. Leaving only enough men and equipment to contain the Dorsey fire,

Several fires came close to claiming the entire city in 1902, convincing officials that there was a need for a more robust water delivery infrastructure. *Courtesy of the Fire Museum of Texas.*

As Dallas buildings grew taller, firefighters faced greater challenges when fighting fires. Long extension ladders were one of the few ways firemen could reach the upper floors. *Courtesy of the Fire Museum of Texas.*

Magee departed for the scene of the new blaze on Lamar Street, between Record and Hord Streets.

The new fire had begun on the roof of a residence, probably sparked by embers from the Dorsey fire. It had jumped to a neighboring residence, then across the alley to another and then across the street to a lumber yard. By the time the exhausted firemen arrived, two city blocks were either smoldering or in flames.

Shorthanded and lacking a full complement of equipment, firefighters could do little but seek to contain the fire. Their ranks were further depleted when thick clouds of smoke from creosote-soaked wood in the lumber yard overcame Chief Magee and three of his firemen. No sooner had the casualties been carried away than another blaze was reported.

What men could be spared—grimy, bruised, exhausted men with cinder holes dotting their blue uniforms and stinking of perspiration and smoke—leaped to their equipment and goaded equally exhausted horses south on a hard run to Fisher Lane, where a block of residences was aflame. The weary firemen had extinguished the Fisher Lane fires by dawn, but seven residences were burned to ashes. The Dorsey Printing Building was a brick shell, and flames still leapt from the Griffith Lumber Company throughout much of the following day.

Insurance adjusters estimated the cost of that "infernal night" to be somewhere north of $500,000, the costliest fire in Dallas history to date. More than two hundred wage earners at the printing plant, lumber yard and other affected businesses lost their jobs. There were no fatalities; Captain Meyers suffered a fractured skull and was eventually able to return to duty. The men who had been overcome by smoke and heat recovered fully.

As bad as the infernal night was, it could have been a lot worse. Had the wind been just a bit brisker, the fire could have gutted most of downtown Dallas. And if the fire hadn't occurred in the early-morning hours, when water use was lowest and commercial cisterns were at their fullest, the flames might not have stopped until they burned to the banks of the Trinity River.

———◆———

DALLAS HAD SEVERAL MORE close calls during the dry summer of 1902. The Music Hall, Exposition Hall, three livestock buildings and four equipment sheds at the state fairgrounds were destroyed in a July fire, when low water pressure hindered firefighting efforts. Seventy-five East Dallas residences burned to the ground in a sweeping fire in June, when firemen couldn't draw sufficient water from the mains. John Clark became the first Dallas firefighter to lose his life in the line of duty as he attempted to slow the fire using chemical retardants and was overcome by the heat.[172]

Insurance carriers hiked premium rates by 10 percent for some and up to 100 percent for others. Most insurers cited lack of water to fight fires and inadequate firefighting equipment as the reasons for their rate increases.[173]

That winter, the city authorized the purchase of firefighting equipment that was better suited to fight fires in multistory buildings. It also directed Chief Magee to investigate some of the new motorized equipment to aid in faster response. At the same time, the city began a multiyear plan to solve its water pressure problem. Block by block, the constricted four-and-a-half-inch water mains were replaced with eight-inch mains. An improved pumping station at the Turtle Creek Water Plant allowed the city to draw

By the end of the 1920s, motor pumpers, a reliable source of water, and larger water mains allowed firefighters to control some of the larger fires. *Courtesy of DeGolyer Library, Southern Methodist University.*

water from the new reservoir at Bachman's Lake, and plans were made to build another reservoir and pumping station on White Rock Creek on the eastern outskirts of the city.[174]

Only by extreme good fortune did twentieth-century Dallas avoid the city-leveling fires that were experienced by Chicago and other cities. But for the first years of the new century, Dallas was a fire trap—one match and one breeze away from total conflagration.

MORE DEADLY CALAMITIES

Regardless of the century or decade, divorces can bring out the worst in people. The Greenberg-Habel hearing in a Dallas courtroom in December 1910 almost resulted in the parents' child being torn in two.[175]

Harry Habel appeared in Judge Young's court, asking permission to visit his four-year-old daughter, whom he had not seen since her infancy and his divorce from the girl's mother. Habel had cost himself custody by stalking and threatening the child's mother and biting off the nose of her new husband. Mrs. Greenberg feared her emotional ex-husband and brought to court a half-dozen aunts, sisters and cousins from her large Polish family for support.

When the judge again denied visitation, Habel, with tears in his eyes, walked into the gallery to hand his child a tin of candy and fruit he had brought her. Afraid that Habel might try to kidnap the child, several of the mother's friends literally jumped on the father's back. Habel was close enough to grab each of the little girl's ankles with his two hands. "Men knocked Habel to the floor, but with the frenzy of a madman, he still clung to the ankles of his baby," a horrified reporter wrote. More women grabbed the infant and pulled her in the opposite direction. "Bystanders declared the little one was stretched until it was five feet long." A bailiff jumped on Habel, smashing his face until his nose was broken and he lost consciousness. Only then did the child slip from his grip.

Once the child was back in her mother's arms, her friends turned on Habel, kicking and cursing him in Polish. Judge Young left the bench to quell the free-for-all, yelling at the women to stop beating the man.

Deputies finally hustled Habel into an office. As the judge cleared the courtroom, Habel could be heard wailing and crying bitterly. Later, Habel apologized to the judge, saying he had so brooded over his troubles that he had not been himself at times.

Judge Young asked the county physician to examine the child for injuries. "Although the muscles of her stomach were strained by the tug of war," the doctor reported, "I do not think the injuries will prove serious." The physician was right about injuries sustained in the courtroom tussle, but little Emma Greenburg's father would cause much more suffering eighteen months later.

"Screaming in an agony of fear as she ran through the rear of a tailoring establishment at 2304 South Ervay yesterday, Mrs. Dora Greenburg was struck three times with bullets from a revolver and dropped dead just outside the door," the *Dallas Morning News* reported. Harry Habel then walked out of the tailor shop, down an alley and into a lumberyard, "where he sent a bullet from a small-caliber revolver smashing through his brain and fell lifeless to the ground."[176] Investigators found seventy dollars and a note in Habel's pocket. "This money is to be paid to Miss Emma Habel when she is of age," the letter said. "Please take my child and place her in a permanent home and raise her up as a lady."

The following day, a brief orthodox ceremony was said over a plain wood casket containing the body of Mrs. Dora Greenberg, followed by burial at the White Rock Jewish Cemetery. Six-year-old Emma, an orphan, lived with her widowed grandmother. By the age of fourteen, Emma had completed school and was a stock clerk at a Dallas department store.[177]

———•———

ALBERT HAWKINS CALLED HIMSELF a painter, but he made his living as a hustler. Thieving, gambling, drinking, playing girls or whatever might earn a little money was his career path. In May 1904, Hawkins was being held in Dallas County Jail on a charge of burglary. (He was caught at night stealing from a home he had painted that day.) On May 3, he was escorted from the jail to the courthouse to testify at trial against another thief, a competitor who Hawkins didn't mind seeing get a lengthy sentence. After Hawkins testified, a bailiff placed him in the sheriff's office while looking for a deputy to escort the prisoner back to jail.[178] That's when Hawkins awarded himself a two-legged parole.

Taking advantage of a moment of inattention, Hawkins leaped out of an open window and sprinted west, toward the Trinity River Bottoms. Deputies Con Gano and Arch Cochran gave chase—Gano down Main Street and Cochran down Elm. Hawkins was trying to cross the river on the Commerce Street Bridge, but on seeing that he was about to be outrun, he zigged to the riverbank and dove in to swim across. Apparently, the hustler didn't recall that he had never learned to swim. Twenty feet from the bank and thrashing to stay afloat, he turned to face the officers on the riverbank. "I don't believe I can make it, boss," he yelled. When he saw their drawn pistols, Hawkins threw both hands into the air, which drove his face underwater. He never came up again.

Deputies procured grab hooks from the fire department and searched the stream for their prisoner. Three days later, Hawkins's body rose to the surface near where he was last seen and floated to the Zang Boulevard crossing. The county coroner reported that he had died as a result of accidental drowning.[179]

———◆———

MILLIONS OF PEOPLE STEP into elevators today, never considering the reliability of the device or their personal safety. Cornelius Otis demonstrated his patented braking elevator in 1856, but the public remained wary of the invention. Forty years later, elevators were still new devices for many and were just coming into use in some of Dallas's taller buildings. Tragically, elevator operation could be a learn-as-you-go skill for some.

The Huey & Phillips Hardware Company installed a freight elevator in its warehouse to help employees move merchandise from floor to floor. Sixty-year-old Rudolph Bachman, a warehouseman, wheeled his order into the elevator on the third floor. When he pulled the lever to lower the lift, he accidentally released the brake, allowing the car to free fall forty-eight feet to the basement.[180] The old man's head was cleaved by a supporting timber, and he died that evening without regaining consciousness.

The Oriental was one of Dallas's first luxury hotels to install an elevator. Joe McCanless, the regular elevator operator, had been training young Neal Mayor as a backup operator. On Wednesday afternoon, July 19, 1904, McCanless, satisfied with his nineteen-year-old trainee's progress, allowed him to make his first solo run.[181] Mayor's first call was a summons from an upper floor. He entered the car but neglected to close the brass folding door.

As the elevator rose, Mayor stuck his head through the gate, striking the top of the opening and jamming his head between the floor of the car and the door casement. McCanless was able to reach into the compartment to release the pressure on Mayor's head, causing Mayor to fall from the car, roll into the shaft and fall to the basement.

When the hotel physician finally reached the boy, he discovered Mayor had "a deep gash in his left temple, left eyeball cut and mashed so that it protruded from its socket, and the tongue almost severed from its root." Mayor was rushed to the hospital, where an examination showed he had broken his jaw as well. Mayor was conscious throughout the ordeal, but attending doctors said they were doubtful he would survive the night.

Thirteen-year-old George Bell operated a bootblack station in the lobby of the Kampmann Building and was well-known in the area. An orphan of uncertain residence, the boy ran errands for tenants, hailed hacks, delivered newspapers in the building and generally made himself useful.[182] When the man who ran the cigar store in the Kampmann lobby dropped a half-dollar and watched it roll down the elevator shaft, Bell offered to help recover it. The elevator operator took Bell to the basement and raised the car several feet to give him a chance to retrieve the coin. Bell snaked himself under the raised car and pulled the shiny Barber

Dallas's City Park was a popular entertainment and recreation destination. Here, a family could listen to music or orators, play with their children or simply stroll the grounds. *Courtesy of DeGolyer Library, Southern Methodist University.*

silver half-dollar from the grease and dirt of the pit. As Bell called out his success, the operator suddenly lowered the car, breaking the bootblack's neck and almost decapitating him. When news of Bell's death reached the Kampmann Building's tenants, they took up a collection to pay his burial expenses.

———◆———

WEATHER AT THE BEGINNING of April 1904 was warm and sunny—perfect for boys playing in City Park. On a late Sunday afternoon, a passerby found ten-year-old Billy Donahue with a hole driven deep into his temple. Doctors determined that a spike of some sort had been driven into the boy's head.[183] Police later learned that the injuries were caused by a playmate who had struck him with a board that had a nail in it. Billy Donahue was the only child of John Donahue, a widower who lived at 262 Masten Street.

———◆———

IN ITS EARLY YEARS, the Dallas Police Department boasted a cadre of mounted police. While that may have provided good policing in an age of horses, buggies and dirt streets, the advent of the automobile required faster, more stable transportation for law enforcers.

South Ervay Street had become a nighttime speedway for automobiles by 1904. Charged with reducing the number of speeders in that residential neighborhood, Policeman J.B. Riddle and his horse hid in an alley to watch out for and apprehend speeding automobile drivers. He didn't have to wait long. "The automobile was going at least thirty-five miles an hour," Riddle said later. "It seemed to be the greatest speed of the kind I have ever noticed before on a street."[184] Riddle and his horse took off in hot pursuit.

"My objective was to see the machine as it passed under a light and so ascertain its driver and its number," he said. Just as the vehicle passed under a light, Riddle's horse lost its footing on the asphalt surface, fell to the ground and rolled over the policeman. The left side of Riddle's head was severely bruised, and a gash had been cut in his temple. Riddle also suffered a severe sprain of his right hip and leg. The policeman came up grinning, however. "I found out who was the driver, and I recorded the number of his machine," Riddle said. The policeman made the arrest but, soon after, traded his horse for a foot beat.

———◆———

JAMES DUROSS LIVED WITH his wife and children in San Marcos but had been working in Dallas for several months, laying track for the Southern Traction Company. In Dallas, he stayed in a boardinghouse at 712 Masten Street. Saturday was Duross's usual wash-up day, but he decided to take his towel and soap down the hall to the washroom on Wednesday, Christmas Eve 1913. Somehow—and police could never quite figure out how—Duross stepped on a cake of soap on the bathroom floor and, slipping, fell out of the second-floor bathroom window. The fall alone would probably not have proven fatal, but Duross fell across a white picket fence below, three pickets penetrating his abdomen and sliding some distance into his innards. Doctors and a carpenter at Parkland Hospital removed the pickets, but it did little to prolong the life of Mr. Duross. Ed C. Smith and Co. handled the funeral arrangements.[185]

———◆———

THE STATE OF TEXAS chooses to execute some felons, and it does so in a carefully prescribed manner. The death penalty is administered only after a rigorous legal process is carried out, involving a trial by jury, a hearing in front of an appeals court and a review by the governor. Finally, the county sheriff acts only after being given a legal order signed by a local district judge. However, from time to time, a different judge would hold court in Texas cities, a judge determined to shorten the process. This judge took his verdicts not from a jury, but from a mob. He was called Judge Lynch, and he was the mob.

Two dozen arson fires burned gins, barns and livestock pens in Hayes County in 1890, leading a newspaper editor to warn that "no surprise need be expressed if Judge Lynch should convene his court in that county shortly." When a confessed murderer escaped conviction on a legal technicality, another newspaper hinted that "the time for dispensing with Judge Lynch's services has not yet come." The newspaper also said that if the law didn't take care of the assassin, "Judge Lynch will take jurisdiction of his case."[186]

In the fall of 1884, Judge Lynch held court in Dallas.

Dallas experienced a rash of home invasion robberies in June 1884. Particularly hard hit were the homes of the wealthy along Ross Avenue. In one night alone, thieves entered three homes to steal valuables while the residents slept. Mrs. W.H. Flippen was alone in her house at 281 Ross Avenue; her husband, a banker and city treasurer, was away on business. Just before daylight on the morning of June 23, she awoke from her bed on the sleeping porch, having heard a noise upstairs. She surprised a large Black man as he rummaged through the drawers of a bureau. Mrs. Flippen screamed loud enough to wake her neighbors before the thief grabbed her and began to choke her into silence. On hearing neighbors running to her aid, the Black man escaped out a window and down an awning post.[187]

By nightfall, the police had arrested a suspect. "The city is alive tonight with armed and determined men ready to lynch the Black fiend who assaulted Mrs. Flippen," said an observer. Five hundred citizens surrounded the building, determined to dispense immediate justice once the victim arrived to identify the man.

The following morning, when Mrs. Flippen viewed the prisoner, she was quite sure he was not the man who had assaulted her. When it became known that the wrong party had been arrested, the excitement died down. The city announced a reward of $500 and assured the public that efforts to capture the man "have not relaxed and are being conducted by officials in a quiet and more orderly way."

Two months later, police arrested William Allen Taylor in Fort Worth for the Ross Avenue robberies and the assault on Mrs. Flippen. "We are confident we have the right Negro," the Dallas sheriff said.[188] Bill Taylor was best known around Dallas as a craps shooter and double-dealer. He had attempted to recruit others to assist him with the June robberies, and those would-be accomplices had turned him in. "If he had a friend in Dallas, even among his own color, it is unknown," a reporter said.

Tempers still ran high regarding Mrs. Flippen's assault (and several others that appeared to be connected.) Hearing rumors that a mob might try to storm the jail and grab his prisoner, Sheriff Smith quietly moved Bill Taylor to the Ellis County jail in Waxahachie. When word leaked out that Taylor was in Ellis County, the sheriff took a wagon and drove back to Waxahachie to move his prisoner once again. Sheriff Smith's intention was to collect Taylor and, together, drive to Midlothian, where they would catch the train to Waco and the county jail there.[189] Smith and his handcuffed prisoner never made it as far as Midlothian. Four miles short of where he expected to meet the Santa Fe train, a group of nine masked and armed men stopped Smith and took his prisoner at gunpoint. The masked men drove Bill Taylor back to Dallas.

By the time they reached Dallas, at nearly 10:00 p.m., the mob had grown to include several hundred individuals. Taylor tried to convince the group that he was innocent, but Judge Lynch had already ruled. The crowd walked Taylor onto the Trinity Bridge, tied one end of a rope around his neck and the other to a wooden railing. With no formal pronouncement, they threw Bill Taylor off the bridge, allowing him to strangle for twenty minutes until all signs of life left him. Taylor's body was allowed to remain hanging overnight for spectators to see the following day; later, a Black minister came to cut him down and bury him.

———•———

"IT IS, NO DOUBT, common in young cities when the flush of new-born prosperity is upon them and everything is going forward with a rush, for buildings to be built the same way," the *Times-Herald*'s editor wrote in 1880. In other words, even a fresh, young city like Dallas can age quickly, particularly if it is not built carefully in the first place.[190] The *Times-Herald* editorial was referring to a building collapse that had occurred on Elm Street the previous day. Without warning, the one-story brick building collapsed just before the lunch hour, sending pedestrians scrambling into the street to avoid the falling brick and masonry. In the years surrounding the turn of the century, buildings were collapsing like wet cardboard, threatening injury and death. Dallas was—and perhaps still is—spotted with aging structures, ready to spill down on those who live in them or walk past them.

Building contractor A. Watson, in 1902, leased a one-story brick building on Elm Street, near Ervay Street, for use as an office while he supervised the construction of the Green Building next door. Watson and two coworkers were working late one evening when they heard a deep creaking and the thuds of heavy objects striking the sidewalk outside. The three men ran out under a rainstorm of bricks and scrambled into the street as their building collapsed behind them.[191]

The St. James Hotel was one of Dallas's most elegant structures in the city's earliest days. One could enter its foyer in the company of generals,

This is the St. James Hotel before it collapsed in 1902. Many residents used a rear exit door when fleeing for safety. *Courtesy of the Dallas Public Library.*

railroad magnates, industrial titans, women with peacock hats, governors and a presidential candidate. By 1902, however, it was decrepit, the lobby dulled by accumulated smoke from thousands of cigars. It was a refuge for pensioners, perspiring salesmen with pressboard sample cases and pay-as-you-go weekly tenants. The building was scheduled for demolition later in the year. But at 2:00 on Monday morning, June 23, 1902, the three-story St. James Hotel collapsed with a crash that was heard for blocks around its location on Main and Murphy Streets. The interior supports gave way, and the building fell in on itself; a tsunami of brick, timber and rubble spilled out into the street, pulling down telephone posts and electric wires with it. Ten occupants were sleeping in upstairs rooms at the time of the collapse. The manager and his family were asleep on the first floor.[192]

The beat cop was first on the scene. He notified his captain and the fire department. The firefighters, including Chief Magee, waded into the unstable rubble to see who might be rescued. "I was awakened by the walls and floors shaking," said James Nolan, whose room was on the third floor.

"I hadn't time to rise from bed before I was carried down under a mass of timber to the basement." Firefighters were able to remove the heavy timbers from across Nolan. N. H. Dillon was another third-floor resident who fell into the basement. Rescuers had trouble finding him, but he remained conscious and was able to direct firefighters to him. Fire Chief Magee located one man on top of the debris stark naked, every stitch having been torn from his body. The man was dazed and couldn't seem to understand why he was sitting on wreckage in the open without his clothes. W.H. Fletcher, the manager, made a speedy exit with his wife and two daughters—all still clad in their nightclothes—through a door from their quarters and into the alley. Though shaken up, he gave the police captain a list of the tenants.

As rescue efforts continued, the Salvation Army set up a tent in a vacant lot next to the wreckage. Alerted to the disaster, twenty local doctors arrived to treat the casualties. Injuries included lacerations, bruises and shock. Mr. J. Rose was the most seriously injured, probably with a broken back, and he was taken to Parkland Hospital for treatment.

By sunrise, only one tenant was unaccounted for, but dawn illuminated a third-floor room that appeared to be unaffected by the collapse. Police and reporters clambered up the wreckage to the door of the untouched room. Several reporters kicked it open and found a man still asleep, completely unaware of the disaster that surrounded him. "It took a good shaking and some choice English (and Irish) to convince the man it was time to move to safer quarters," one of the reporters noted.

"The escapes of the occupants from instant death under tons of brick and timber is considered miraculous in the extreme and entirely without precedent," the *Dallas Daily Herald* reported. In truth, it was just another deadly day in Dallas.

STILL DEADLY

L ive as if you expected to live a hundred years, but might die tomorrow," wrote Ann Lee, founder of the Shaker sect, almost two centuries ago. *Deadly Dallas* demonstrates how fleeting life could be—and how transitory it might be today, too.

The events in this book occurred more than one hundred years ago. A century later, we may believe that we are smarter, better equipped and better prepared to avoid these calamities. But a surprise nighttime tornado tore through Dallas in 2019, smashing schools, businesses and homes. In 2007, fiery gas canisters pelted a busy freeway following an explosion at a welding gas plant. A 2018 natural gas explosion killed a child, flattened a house and required a section of North Dallas to be replumbed due to faulty gas piping. More than two hundred lives were lost in traffic accidents in Dallas in 2017, most of them due to speed, alcohol and inattention. And at its peak in 2020, more than twenty people a day were dying in a viral epidemic.

There may be some dark humor in the manner of demise of individuals at the turn of the twentieth century. It may seem silly that no one thought to establish strict traffic laws when the automobile first appeared on Dallas streets. Didn't people know that unvaccinated dogs running loose could spread rabies? And why on earth would anyone allow dynamite to be sold by the stick at the local hardware store? Imagine, though, the people of a century from now looking back at the manner of deaths today. Whether it's life at the turn of the twentieth century, the twenty-first or the twenty-second, Dallas will still be deadly. Perhaps it's best to live as if we expect to live one hundred years but to know we might still encounter those unfortunate incidents, grievous mayhem or grisly fatalities at any time.

ACKNOWLEDGEMENTS

Deadly Dallas was born from a series of talks at the annual *Legacies* Dallas History Conferences in 2018 and 2020. Historian and editor Michael V. Hazel was kind enough to publish articles based on these talks in *Legacies*, a history journal for Dallas and North Central Texas.

Ben Gibson, commissioning editor of The History Press, recognized the potential of *Deadly Dallas*. He and the professional editorial, production and marketing staffs at The History Press guided me through every step of the publication process.

Much of this book was written at a booth in a friendly diner that's as plain and unassuming as its name: J's Breakfast & Burgers. Thanks to Mike and the rest of the staff for keeping my cup topped off and the flattop grill sizzling hot.

Six trusted individuals read an early version of this manuscript. They provided thoughtful, literate and honest comments about what they read. B.J. Austin, Mary Jean Hilton, Janie Kizer, Ginger Hendrix, Vrena Patrick and Rodger F. Whitney helped sharpen the narrative and protect me from some of my own excesses.

Author Mike Cox is a Texas treasure, and I'm fortunate to have him as an inspiration, adviser, coach and friend.

This is my sixth book, and there are some special people who've been supportive and encouraging from the first: Crystal Kreitzer, Dr. Chris Gallup, Chuck Larson and Joanie and Gary Cox. For the last several years, two tireless guys—David Laredo and Scott Seybold—have accompanied me on research trips and have gone to book talks and to out-of-the-way Texas destinations. They call themselves "roadies." I call them lifelong friends.

My sister and brother-in-law, Ann John and Brien, graciously provided a spare bedroom and a comfortable writing nook when I ventured to the Texas Hill Country. Pat Williams, Julian Fletcher, Meagan Alma and Ava Kai are always on my mind.

A NOTE ON SOURCES

The stories of the people and events described in *Deadly Dallas* come from primary sources. I mainly relied on coverage published in the *Dallas Morning News* and the *Dallas Herald*. Additionally, I referred to contemporary city directories and insurance maps. When other area newspapers of the time provided details that were not reported in the local newspapers, I used those as well. All sources are clearly cited in the chapter notes.

From time to time, I consulted current sources for historical context or data. These secondary sources are also cited in the chapter notes.

Much of *Deadly Dallas* was written at a time when libraries and archives were closed to researchers due to COVID-19. Digitized newspaper pages (and other digital documents) were available due to the efforts of such institutions as Dallas Public Library, SMU Libraries Digital Collections, Library of Congress Chronicling America and the HathiTrust Digital Library.

One of the most comprehensive and easily searchable digital archives of Texas history is UNT's Portal to Texas History. The portal has digitized almost two million items of Texas history: newspapers, city directories, maps, postcards, letters, photographs, yearbooks and much more. Access to much of the material cited in *Deadly Dallas* was possible due to the Portal to Texas History.

Despite closures and reassignments due to effects of the pandemic, professionals from a dozen institutions helped research and provide the images that appear in *Deadly Dallas*. The images are identified by source in the text. The DeGolyer Library, Southern Methodist University, provided images from the George W. Cook Dallas/Texas Image Collection and the SMU Student Newspapers Collection. The Fire Museum of Texas, located in Beaumont, provided images 1986-01-0-66-01, 1986-01-1-74-01, 1986-01-2-15-01, 1986-01-2-28-01, 1986-01-2-51-01 and 1986-01-2-53-01. The image from the University of North Texas Special Collections came from the Clark Family Photography Collection. The University of Texas at Arlington provided an image from the *Fort Worth Star-Telegram* Collection, Special Collections. The University of Texas at Dallas provided images from the William G. Fuller and Ormer Locklear Collections, Special Collections and Archives Division, Eugene McDermott Library. The Dallas History and Archives Division of the Dallas Public Library provided images. Additional images came from Anderson County Historical Commission, Clay County Historical Society, Historic Mesquite Inc. and Hardin-Simmons University Libraries.

All images have been used with permission.

NOTES

Chapter 1

1. "One of Dallas' Constant Perils," *Dallas Daily Herald* (hereafter cited as *DTH*), August 30, 1897.
2. "Thrilling Runaway," *DTH*, August 30, 1897.
3. "Constant Perils," *DTH*.
4. "Instructions Given Police," *Dallas Morning News* (hereafter cited as *DMN*), April 17, 1906.
5. "Passengers and Mules Pulled Together in Old Days of Car Service on Dallas Streets," *DTH*, June 11, 1922.
6. Mrs. Hurley later sued the transit company for negligence and received $20,000 in damages for medical expense and the loss of her husband ("Street Car Accident," *DMN*, August 31, 1892). "Bench and Bar," *DTH*, July 21, 1893.
7. "A Collision Avoided," *DMN*, April 30, 1889.
8. "History of Local Street Car System From Mules to Skip-Stop is Romance," *DTH*, July 13, 1919.
9. Mule service: "The Street Railway System," *DTH*, September 6, 1899. Electric service: *Street Railway Journal* (March 1892): 144.
10. "Boy Mangled and Crushed," *DMN*, July 27, 1900.
11. "Fireman Coffman Injured," *DMN*, October 26, 1902.
12. "Killed by Cars," *DMN*, April 27, 1907.
13. "Funeral of Geeson," *DMN*, April 28, 1907.

14. Accidents like these proved expensive for the transit companies. In April 1904, a *Dallas Daily Herald* reporter happened by the electric railway business office to find two supervisors examining a list of damage suits for the first three months of the year. "The sum could not be included in less than six figures," the reporter noted ("Damage Suits Are Numerous," *DTH*, April 18, 1904).

15. "A Disastrous Collision," *DMN*, October 15, 1899.

16. "Underground Sidewalks," *DMN*, March 30, 1902.

17. "Thousands in Dallas," *DTH*, September 13, 1903.

18. An interview with Green and his description of the drive can be found at "Mr. E.H.R. Green's Carriage," *DMN*, October 6, 1899.

19. Green remained an enthusiastic motorist. He was an organizer and first president of the Dallas Automobile Club and a board chairman of the Texas State Automobile Association.

20. "Runaway's Bad Results," *DMN*, April 28, 1904.

21. "Automobiles," *DMN*, January 1, 1905; D.C. Greer, *History of the Texas Highway Department*, rev. ed. (Austin: Texas Highway Department, Information and Statistics Division, 1959); "Annual Report of the State Highway Commission," 1924.

22. "Four Vehicles in Collision," *DMN*, April 23, 1912.

23. "'Jay-Walker' Fined $2," *DMN*, August 16, 1914.

24. "E.E. Hall Is Run Over and Killed by Taxicab," *DMN*, September 26, 1909.

25. "Auto Speeding Case Heard," *DMN*, November 14, 1907.

26. "Protest Against Speeding," *DMN*, November 16, 1907.

27. "Dallas Auto Club," *DMN*, June 24, 1904; "Application for Charter," *DMN*, July 2, 1904.

28. "Automobile Bill," *DMN*, February 3, 1905; "Case Heard," *DMN*.

29. "Need for Traffic Regulations in Dallas Is Shown Daily," *DMN*, November 24, 1910.

30. "Traffic Regulations Proposed for Dallas," *DMN*, November 6, 1910.

31. "Grand Jury Inquiry for Auto Accident" and "Severe Penalty for Speeding," *DMN*, April 24, 1912.

32. "Woman Killed by Automobile Is Identified," *DTH*, November 25, 1920.

33. "Jess Hassell Is Released on Bond," *DMN*, December 2, 1920; "Killing Woman Cost Hassell over $10,000," *Texas Mesquiter*, April 1, 1921.

34. James B. Jacobs, *Drunk Driving: An American Dilemma* (Chicago: University of Chicago Press, 2013); E. Behr, *Prohibition. Thirteen Years That Changed America* (New York: Arcade, 1996).

35. "Hassell Is Charged with Aggravated Assault," *DMN*, February 25, 1921; "Jess Hassell Fined $100 Each on Two Charges," *DMN*, April 5, 1921; "Restrain Jess Hassell from Operating Car," *DTH*, December 13, 1921.
36. "Jess Hassell Is Given New Trial," *DMN*, February 5, 1922. At some point in his later life, Hassell stopped drinking. When he died in 1954, he was vice president of Oak Cliff Bank & Trust and had a sterling reputation ("Jess Hassell, Ex-Baseball Chief, Dies," *DMN*, March 3, 1954).
37. "A Clearing House for Petty Crimes," *DMN*, April 4, 1925.
38. "Traffic Deaths Discredit City," *DMN*, December 18, 1930.

Chapter 2

39. "She Froze to Death," *DMN*, March 19, 1896.
40. "The Fate of Amos Christian, a Well-Known Dallas Darky," *DMN*, March 25, 1882.
41. "Man Heavily Clad Is Found Dead in Cold," *DMN*, January 7, 1912.
42. Boyce House, *I Give You Texas* (San Antonio, TX: Naylor Co., 1943).
43. National Weather Service, "History of the National Weather Service," www.weather.gov.
44. The *Farmers' Almanac* is still published annually, still larded with recipes, folklore, gardening tips and astrological calendars. The "Foster's Weather Bulletin" column appeared in some Texas newspapers off and on between 1906 and 1930.
45. *Isaac's Storm* by Erik Larson (New York: Crown, 1999) is a quite readable true account of the Galveston hurricane told through the personal story of a U.S. Weather Bureau employee there.
46. "Wrecked by a Cyclone," *DMN*, August 24, 1907.
47. "Injured by Cyclone," *DMN*, February 4, 1903; "Dallas Storm Swept," *Orange Daily Tribune*, June 3, 1904.
48. Local newspapers published detailed accounts of the storm ("Shattered the City's Suburbs," *DTH*, January 20, 1894; "After the Cyclone," *DTH*, January 21, 1894; "Swept by Wind," *DMN*, January 21, 1894).
49. "Weather in Dallas," *DMN*, November 17, 1902.
50. "Sleighing and Coasting," *DMN*, February 6, 1905.
51. "A Heavy Snow Storm," *DMN*, February 15, 1895.
52. "Heaviest Snow in Nineteen Years," *DMN*, February 18, 1910.
53. "Sunstroke. Unparalleled Heat—The Thermometer Ranges from 108 to 114 in the Shade!," *Dallas Weekly Herald*, August 5, 1876.

54. "Alone in the Field," *DTH*, July 21, 1892; Biographical information from minutes of the Confederate Association of Kentucky, Louisville Public Library.

55. "Thunderstorm Does Damage in Dallas," *DMN*, August 4, 1914.

Chapter 3

56. "A Lamp Explosion," *DTH*, October 13, 1892.

57. "Burned to Death," *DTH*, July 29, 1899.

58. "Fate of the Farnhams," *DMN*, July 30, 1899.

59. "Dynamite Blows Man to Top of Well," *Fort Worth Star-Telegram*, May 19, 1904.

60. "Found Dying in His Room," *DMN*, June 6, 1886.

61. "Child Is Made Bind by Dynamite Explosion," *El Paso Herald*, August 9, 1919.

62. "Exploding of Dynamite Kills Boys Handling It," *DMN*, February 18, 1909.

63. "Whole City Was Shocked," *DTH*, July 24, 1903; "Shocks Entire Town," *DMN*, July 25, 1903.

64. "Man Blown to Bits in Dynamite Explosion," *DTH*, April 7, 1914.

65. "Explosion Foils Robbery," (San Antonio) *Daily Express*, December 29, 1909.

66. "Broken Rail Is Discovered," *DMN*, March 2, 1910.

67. "Dynamite on Track Again," *DTH*, March 8, 1910; "Steel Rail Damaged on Interurban Track," *DMN*, March 9, 1910.

68. "Dynamite Under Sherman Road," *DMN*, April 20, 1910.

69. "Interurban Track Blown Up," *DMN*, May 3, 1910.

70. "Jungleland Wrecked by Terrific Explosion," *DTH*, January 11, 1912.

71. The description and promotional language come from an advertisement: "Jungleland Picture House," *DMN*, July 12, 1912.

72. "Gas Causes Big Explosion," *Lancaster Herald*, January 19, 1912.

73. "Building Was Badly Damaged," *DTH*, January 12, 1912; "Gas Explosion in Dallas," *Bryan Eagle and Pilot*, January 11, 1912.

74. "Teacher Meets Horrible Death in Gas Explosion," *Dallas Express*, February 10, 1923; "Negro Teacher Is Burned to Death," *DMN*, February 6, 1923.

75. "Funeral of the Late Miss Gladys V. Hurdle of Dallas," *Dallas Express*, February 17, 1923.

76. Thorough newspaper coverage and photographs of the event can be found in the *Dallas Morning News* and *Dallas Times Herald* from May 12, 1927. See also "Blast Killing 6 Ascribed to Escaping Gas" and "Larger Emergency Hospital Favored," *DMN*, May 13, 1927.

77. "Man Is Killed in Explosion," *DMN*, July 2, 1927; "Three Injured as Empty Gas Tank Explodes," (Timpson) *Weekly Times*, July 8, 1927.

78. "Damage Suit Follows Truck Explosion," *DMN*, July 6, 1927.

79. "Gas and Dynamite Threaten Explosion," *Borger Daily Herald*, April 4, 1927.

80. "Is Scalded to Death by Boiler Explosion," *DMN*, May 21, 1911.

81. "Boiler Explosion, One Dead, One Hurt," *DMN*, July 20, 1911; "Injuries Are Fatal to Mrs. C.C. Cormack," *DMN*, July 21, 1911 (the news misspelled the Carmack's last name throughout their coverage). For more information about the farm family, see "Mesquite People Victims of Terrible Accident," *Texas Mesquite*, July 21, 1911, and "Mrs. Carmack Follows Husband to the Grave," *Texas Mesquite*, July 28, 1911.

82. The *Dallas Morning News* published stories about the well and the reluctant nitro through much of early February 1888. See "The Artesian Well," *DMN*, February 4, 1888; "Shooting the Well," *DMN*, February 7, 1888; and "Local Notes," *DMN*, February 12, 1888.

Chapter 4

83. "Two Boys Lose Arms When Bomb Explodes," *DMN*, July 5, 1912.

84. "Two Boys Lose Their Arms," *DTH*, July 5, 1912.

85. "Lightning Kills Two of Five Dallas Boys as They Are Planning a Birthday Party," *DMN*, June 2, 1923.

86. This partial listing comes from an order of march that was published in the *Dallas Morning News* on May 30, 1916.

87. "Other Towns Will Join in Parade," *DMN*, May 23, 1916.

88. "Accident Halts 20,000 Citizens in Preparedness Demonstration," *DMN*, May 31, 1916.

89. "Four Killed and Fourteen Injured When Awning Falls During Parade," *DMN*, May 31, 1916.

90. "Another Victim of Accident," *DMN*, June 8, 1916.

91. I've drawn my description of this event from several sources. "Home Hanging," *DTH*, and "The Death Penalty," *Galveston Daily News*, both of August 28, 1880, published separate accounts of Allen Wright's execution.

For details about the process and atmosphere of a Dallas hanging, I've referred to "The Gallows," *DTH*, August 12, 1876, an account of the execution of Wesley Jones. Like that of Wright's, the 1876 hanging was a public one at the same location in the Trinity River Bottoms, presided over by the same sheriff and using the same rope and gallows.

Chapter 5

92. "The Flying Machine," *DMN*, July 27, 1894; "To Test His Airship," *DMN*, March 7, 1901.
93. "Lives Lost in Effort to Conquer the Air with Flying Machines," *DTH*, January 1, 1911. Those four famed aviators would be dead in flying crashes by the end of 1910.
94. "Willi Try to Get Wright Brothers to Come Here," *DMN*, June 20, 1909.
95. "'Daredevil' Brodie Is to Fly in Dallas," *DMN*, March 1, 1910.
96. "First Aeroplane Flights Here Today," *DMN*, March 3, 1910.
97. "Short Flight Made in an Aeroplane," *DMN*, March 4, 1910.
98. "Aeroplane Wrecked and Aviator Hurt," *DMN*, March 6, 1910. Though he kept trying, Brodie would never become a top-tier showman. The timid flyer was killed in 1913 while flying at forty-five feet. His plane flipped, and he was trapped under the engine ("Fall Kills Pioneer Flyer," *New York Times*, April 20, 1913).
99. "Aviation Meet Planned Here," *DMN*, October 24, 1910.
100. "Two World-Famous Aviators Killed," *DMN*, January 1, 1911; "Dallas Aviation Meet Begins Today," *DMN*, January 4, 1911.
101. "Flies over the City at Great Height," *DMN*, January 7, 1911.
102. "Falls from Second Story," *DMN*, January 8, 1911; "Three Amateur Aviators Hurt," *DMN*, January 22, 1911.
103. "Aviation in Dallas," *Aerial Age Weekly*, April 24, 1916.
104. "The Aero Club of Dallas," *Aeronautics* 9, no. 2 (February 1911).
105. "Two Texas Airplanes," *Lancaster Herald*, June 2, 1911. Thirty years after McCarroll's death, Sam Acheson wrote that McCarroll had invented and flown a motorized aircraft in Dallas, mere months after the Wrights first flew at Kitty Hawk, but there is scant evidence for that claim ("McCarroll Pioneered Aviation," *DMN*, May 8, 1967); McCarroll's retractable landing gear was granted U.S. Patent #1,152,743.
106. "Waco Boy Constructs Airship in Dallas," *DMN*, March 24, 1912.
107. "Among the Aviators," *Aero & Hydro*, October 5, 1912.

108. "War Proving a Boon to Aero Activity in Texas," *Aerial Age Weekly*, June 21, 1915.

109. "One of Man's Most Deadly Inventions," *DMN*, December 6, 1913.

110. "Lives Lost," *DTH*.

111. "Brodie First Flyer in Dallas," *DMN*, April 22, 1913.

112. "Killed at College Park MD," *Aerial Age Weekly*, October 29, 1917.

113. "Lincoln Beachey Adds More Loops to Record," *DMN*, November 2, 1914; "Lincoln Beachey Plunged 3,000 Feet to Death in Sea," *Houston Post*, March 16, 1915.

114. "Lieut. Harry Peyton Dies of Hurts in Fall," *DMN*, April 2, 1918.

115. "Opposed to Trip in Air," *DMN*, October 23, 1915.

116. "Aviator Killed by Fall Near Dallas," *DMN*, May 7, 1916.

117. "Aviation," *Aerial Age Weekly*.

118. "14 Aeroplanes in Dallas," *DMN*, April 11, 1916.

119. "Foreign Report," *Aerial Age Weekly*, May 3, 1915.

120. National World War I Museum and Memorial, "Filling the Ranks," www.theworldwar.org; "Dallas Is Selected for Aviation Camp," *DMN*, August 12, 1917.

121. "Love Field Aviator Meets Death in Fall," *DMN*, January 6, 1918; "Honor Dead Flier," *San Antonio Express*, February 7, 1918.

122. "Bay State Aviator Is Killed at Love Field," *Houston Post*, February 20, 1918.

123. Stall: "Love Field Cadet Loses Life in Fall," *DMN*, February 26, 1918; Insinger/Zinn: "Aviator at Love Field Killed in Air Crash," *San Antonio Express*, April 10, 1918; Bidwell: "Aviators Fly Over Train Bearing Body of Comrade," *DMN*, August 4, 1918; Hyde: "Aviator Killed Near Dallas," *Temple Telegram*, August 29, 1918; Bruce/Sego: "Two Love Field Aviators Killed," *DMN*, September 13, 1918.

124. "Dickman's Son Killed in Fall," *New York American*, January 4, 1919.

125. "Lieut. Edward M. Anderson Loses Life in Making Landing at Love Field," *DMN*, July 26, 1919; "Aviator Killed at Love Field," *DMN*, November 8, 1920.

126. See Darwin Payne and Kathy Fitzpatrick, *From Prairie to Planes* (Dallas, TX: Three Forks Press, 1999) for a detailed history of flight operations in Dallas, culminating in the creation of DFW Airport. I relied on pages 22–28 to help me tell Love Field's military history.

127. "Local Flyer Killed in Fall of 500 Feet," *DMN*, October 20, 1919.

128. "Locklear Thrills Movie Fans at the Washington Theater," *DTH*, May 11, 1920.

129. The title character played by Robert Redford in *The Great Waldo Pepper* (1975) was reportedly based on Locklear. For more information on this fascinating flyer, see the Ormer Locklear Collection, Eugene McDermott Library, University of Texas at Dallas.
130. "Girl Finds Bucking Plane Tougher Than Breaking Bronchos," *DMN*, May 8, 1922.
131. "Miss Lillian Boyer Will Perform at Fair Today," *DMN*, October 27, 1922.
132. "Privileges for Sales," classification, *DMN*, August 27, 1916.
133. "Sky's the Limit for Flying Sooners: Oklahomans Leave Indelible Mark on Aviation, Space History," (Oklahoma City) *Oklahoman*, November 15, 1987; "Spotlight of the Week," (Chickasha, OK) *Express-Star*, August 8, 1914. (This was a time when not-so-well-known flyers appropriated names of better-known elite European flyers. Miller didn't take it that far, but "Lestere" certainly sounded more European. For more examples of flyer fakery, see "Aviation's Fakes and Fakirs," *Aeronautics*, September 1912.)
134. "Members of Hood's Brigade Are Arriving at Calvert," *Galveston Daily News*, June 6, 1913; "Old Settlers Gather Today," (Coleman) *Democrat-Voice*, October 3, 1913; "Christmas Trade Days at Electra December 19," *Wichita Weekly Times*, December 18, 1914.
135. "Aeroplane Fails to Fly Because of High Winds," (Weatherford) *Daily Herald*, July 5, 1912; "Local and Personal," (Mesquite) *Texas Mesquiter*, July 6, 1917.
136. "Dallas Aviator Keeps Cool Head in Danger," *DMN*, October 11, 1913.
137. "Big Savings for You!" advertisement, *DMN*, October 2, 1959; "Texas Air Pioneer, Lestere Miller, Dies," *DMN*, February 16, 1963.
138. "Opinion," *DMN*, October 21, 1919.
139. "Lt. Col. Stuart Named New AF Deputy Chief for FW," *Convairiety*, July 6, 1949.
140. "Hunter B. Temple Killed and Two Hurt in Airplane," *DMN*, April 15, 1924; "Girl Hurt in Plane Crash May Survive," *DMN*, April 16, 1924; "Student Killed—One Hurt in Crash," *Semi-Weekly Campus*, April 16, 1924.
141. Federal Aviation Administration, "History," www.faa.gov.

Chapter 6

142. City of Dallas Health Department Collection, Texas/Dallas History & Archives, Dallas Public Library.

143. "City Scavenger Notice," *DTH*, May 29, 1885.

144. "Council Proceedings," *DMN*, June 26, 1887; (No headline), *DMN*, July 1, 1887.

145. "City Laws and Official Publications," *DMN*, October 18, 1894;

146. "Scavenger Contract Not Awarded by City," *DMN*, January 7, 1913.

147. "Fish Poisoned," *DMN*, February 2, 1887.

148. "Would Stifle a Buzzard," *DTH*, October 3, 1891.

149. The *Dallas Morning News* reprinted and explained the report in installments over three consecutive days. For the first, see "Death Lurks Along the Trinity," *DMN*, July 12, 1925.

150. "The Problem with Animal Waste," *Los Angeles County Department of Public Health Newsletter* (June–July 2011).

151. "Commission Meeting Held This Morning," *DTH*, July 19, 1902.

152. "Good Business in Dog Tags," *DMN*, June 13, 1907.

153. "Cases of Rabies Here Show Marked Decrease," *DMN*, March 8, 1924; "Seven Rabies Cases Treated by Doctor," *DMN*, June 12, 1926.

154. "Guard Against Cholera," *DMN*, September 2, 1892; "Problem of Public Health," *DMN*, May 14, 1899; City of Dallas Health Department Collection, Texas/Dallas History & Archives, Dallas Public Library.

155. The dates given in this section come from "Significant Dates in the History of Public Health in Dallas," published as part of the *Researcher's Guide* in the Dallas Health Department Collection, Texas/Dallas History & Archives, Dallas Public Library.

156. Ted Dealey, *Diaper Days of Dallas* (Nashville, TN: Abingdon Press, 1966), 111.

157. "Measles Epidemic Spreads," *Denton Record Chronicle*, February 28, 1924.

158. "Many Deaths from Meningitis," *DMN*, January 1, 1912.

159. "Local Deaths," *DMN*, December 31, 1911.

160. "Schools Not to Open Today," *DMN*, January 2, 1912; "Reassigns Criminal Docket," *DMN*, January 10, 1912.

161. "Siege of Meningitis," *Cordell* (OK) *Herald Sentinel*, December 25, 1911; "Says, No 'Epidemic' in Dallas," *DMN*, January 12, 1912.

Chapter 7

162. "Two Burned Early Today," *DTH*, April 14, 1909.

163. "Explosion Burns Two; One Dead, One May Die," *DMN*, April 15, 1909.

164. "Mrs. Vesta Boatner Is Fatally Burned," *DMN*, July 31, 1914.
165. "Burial to Be in Mississippi," *DMN*, August 1, 1914.
166. "Burned to Death," *DMN*, December 21, 1891.
167. "Burns Fatal to Small Girl Today," *DTH*, August 5, 1914.
168. "Two Children Dead as a Result of Fire," *DMN*, August 6, 1914.
169. "Swept by Fire," *DMN*, March 7, 1902.
170. "Death at a Fire," *DMN*, March 19, 1902.
171. "Great Fires Rage," *DMN*, April 21, 1902.
172. "Dallas Again Visited by Big Conflagration," *DTH*, July 9, 1902; "Pyramid of Flame," *DMN*, July 21, 1902.
173. "Insurance Rates," *DMN*, June 20, 1902.
174. "Water Situation," *DMN*, July 20, 1902.

Chapter 8

175. "Baby Is Almost Torn in Two in Court Room Row," *San Antonio Light*, December 10, 1910.
176. "Kills Former Wife and Ends Own Life," *DMN*, May 3, 1912.
177. "Funeral for Mrs. Greenberg," *DMN*, May 4, 1912.
178. "Drowned in the Trinity," *DTH*, May 4, 1904; "Prisoner Is Drowned," *DMN*, May 4, 1904.
179. "Negro's Body Found," *DMN*, May 8, 1904.
180. "Killed in an Elevator," *DTH*, September 12, 1895.
181. "Accident in an Elevator," *DTH*, July 20, 1904.
182. "Search for Coin Leads to Death of Negro Youth," *San Antonio Express*, September 5, 1908.
183. "Boy's Injury Fatal," *Fort Worth Star-Telegram*, April 5, 1904.
184. "Policeman Falls from Horse," *DMN*, February 18, 1908.
185. "Fall from Bathroom Fatal," *DMN*, December 26, 1913; (No headline), (Coleman) *Democrat-Voice*, January 2, 1914.
186. (No headline), *Brenham Daily Banner*, January 4, 1890; (No headline), *Gainesville Daily Hesperian*, August 29, 1889; (No headline), *Galveston Daily News*, September 17, 1889.
187. "Dallas Excited," *Galveston Daily News*, June 26, 1884; "Should Swing," *DTH*, July 3, 1884.
188. "Notes from Dallas," *Galveston Daily News*, September 5, 1884.
189. I've described the lynching based on accounts published in three newspapers. The details vary somewhat, but I've chosen the parts that

seem most likely. See "Swung to A Limb," *Galveston Daily News*, September 13, 1884; "The Recent Taylor Lynching," *Galveston Daily News*, September 14, 1884; "Judge Lynch," *DTH*, September 18, 1884; and "Notes," *Norton's Union Intelligencer*, September 19, 1884.

190. "Unsafe Buildings," *DTH*, April 2, 1880.

191. "Collapse of Building," *DMN*, May 16, 1902.

192. For accounts of the St. James Hotel collapse, see "Hotel Collapse Injures Several," *DTH*, June 23, 1902, and "A Building Falls," *DMN*, June 23, 1902. For follow-up details and a photograph of the wreckage, see "Only One in Danger," *DMN*, June 24, 1902.

ABOUT THE AUTHOR

Rusty Williams is an award-winning writer-historian who writes about history through the stories of the people who lived it. He is a former journalist who has written for the *Dallas Morning News*, *Fort Worth Star-Telegram*, *San Antonio Express-News* and the Associated Press.

Rusty is the author of *Red River Bridge War: A Texas-Oklahoma Border Battle* (Texas A&M Press), *My Old Confederate Home: A Respectable Place for Civil War Veterans* (University Press of Kentucky), *Historic Photos of Dallas in the 1950s, 1960s, and 1970s* (Turner Publishing) and other books and articles about Texas and the Southwest. He speaks to clubs and organizations throughout the Southwest.

Rusty lives in Dallas. You can reach him through his website, www.rustywilliamsauthor.com or at rustywilliams2004@yahoo.com.

Visit us at
www.historypress.com